DIVE
IN
D.E.E.P.

**STRATEGIES TO ADVANCE YOUR CAREER,
FIND BALANCE, AND LIVE YOUR BEST LIFE**

JOANIE BILY

For my children and the child in all of us.

Chase & Ashley – Dream big, work hard, and always dive into life!

Praise for *Dive In D.E.E.P.*

"Joanie gives readers clear and proven strategies to be more confident, intentional, and empowered to focus on the things that truly matter, and ultimately reach their full potential. I believe she has delivered a must-have resource for students, recent graduates, seasoned leaders, and everyone in between looking to advance their career and live their best life."

– Molly Fletcher, "Hailed as the Female Jerry McGuire" by CNN, Host of Game Changes Podcast, World's Top 50 Keynote Speaker and Author

"Joanie is an exceptional leader who combines deep insight into today's labor market with a fierce passion for championing people to unlock their greatest potential. Her book, *Dive in D.E.E.P.* couldn't have arrived at a better time as the world of work is undergoing vast transformation, and people are increasingly searching for a meaningful, balanced career and life."

– Billy Milam, CEO, Employbridge

"With *Dive in D.E.E.P.*, Joanie has written an authentic, applicable, and powerful guide to thriving personally and professionally. She shares inspirational stories, real-life examples, and exceptional insight into today's labor and career development trends. Her D.E.E.P. process and strategies help guide readers to design a career action plan grounded in confidence and clarity, with advice that extends beyond the workplace to achieve a full, balanced life."

– Bob Nardelli, former Chairman & CEO of Chrysler Corporation & The Home Depot, and founder of XLR-8 LLC

"Dive in D.E.E.P. is a must read. After decades spent working with Joanie in the staffing and recruiting industry, I still seek her out for her impactful, straightforward, and instructive career advice! She is a leader who authentically inspires you to believe and empowers you to turn that belief into a reality. I am elated she is now sharing her indispensable wisdom with the world."

– Joyce Russell, President, Adecco Group US Foundation, Author, *Put a Cherry on Top*, and former Chair of the American Staffing Association

CONTENTS

Strategy 1: **D**esign: Your Approach

Strategy 2: **E**xperience: Use the Springboard

Strategy 3: Execute: Take Off & Fly High

Strategy 4: Persevere: Make a Rip Entry

INTRODUCTION
DIVE IN

"Dive in," my dad said. "I'm right here, and I'll grab you as soon as you hit the water."

Fearful, I stood at the end of the diving board, gazing apprehensively at the deep end of my Aunt Kay's pool.

My dad had always been a great swimmer and diver. My three sisters and I loved to watch him dive off the diving board. We would call out to him: "Do a swan dive!" or "How about a jack knife dive?" My father would play along and show off his impressive diving skills. Of course, we would always rate him a perfect 10. Sadly, I did not inherit his diving techniques.

I was about six years old, and at the time my family didn't have a pool in our small backyard in Queens, New York. So, every summer, my parents would pack up the station wagon and take my sisters and me to New Jersey for a special summer barbecue at Aunt Kay's house. It was always a fun day we all looked forward to—not only for the chance to feast on some of Aunt Kay's famous macaroni salad, but also for the chance to play in the pool all day long.

The previous year's barbecue bash had been a great time, despite my sister Diana and I never leaving the shallow end of the pool for fear of sinking in the deep end. This year, I vowed I was going to learn to swim in the deep end.

When we arrived at Aunt Kay's house, many of my cousins were already in the pool. I wasted no time, quickly changing into my bathing suit and heading out the sliding glass doors to join them. I walked over to the deep end with excitement and jumped up on the diving board. This was it. The moment I had been waiting for. I walked to the edge of the board. But suddenly, my excitement and confidence were quickly replaced by all-out fear. I froze. Maybe this wasn't such a great idea. The pool looked so deep and large. How would I ever be able to dive in and swim to the other side?

"Come on, Joanie!" my dad encouraged. "You've been dreaming about this for weeks. Just go for it. I'm right here, and I promise I will grab you and bring you to the side of the pool. You can do it. Dive in."

I was possessed by a familiar feeling, one I have now come to understand: an overwhelming feeling where I say, "YES, I want to do this," and, "YES, I'm scared" at the same time. Fight or flight. I like to say the "or" becomes an "and" for me. In other words: fight *and* flight.

I finally decided it was time. I had to go for it. So, I did what my dad told me. I stood on the balls of my feet at the end of the diving board, and I started to bounce up and down just a little bit. I pointed my hands downward, tucked my head in, and pushed off the diving board. It was the most beautiful belly flop of all time.

As I hit the water, I was filled with excitement and fear of making it to the side of the pool. In my mind, I kept thinking, *my dad's going to grab me any second.* I kept swimming, but I didn't see my father. Miraculously, I made it to the edge of the pool. When I came up for air, I was mad.

"Dad, you said you were going to help me!" I whined. "Where were you?"

"Joanie, I was right here the whole time," he said, a huge grin painted his face. "You don't need my help. You got this!"

My hands clung to the edge of the pool for a moment, stunned. I was holding on for dear life. But then I realized: *Wait a minute, I just dove into the pool and swam to the other side. I did it!* I spent the rest of the day going down the slide and diving off the diving board in the deep end of the pool.

When I think back to that memorable first dive into the deep end, I see now that it would become a striking metaphor for how I approach my career and life. I had dreamt of diving into the deep end, and I took a chance, despite the fear and hesitation to achieve that goal. I realized at an early age that if I take risks and put in the effort, I can accomplish my aspirations. I can achieve my dreams, so long as I continue to push myself out of my comfort zone and build and practice new skills. I found out that if I want something badly enough, I need to be willing to work for it and make it happen.

Finally, I learned that when I reach my goal, I need to have fun and enjoy the moment.

Sounds easy, right? Yet, many of us hold ourselves back, afraid to dive in and take the risk. Having spent 25 years in the staffing and recruiting industry, I've worked with hundreds of employers and thousands of job seekers imparting career advice at every turn. It's in my DNA. So, naturally, my goal with this book is to help people build and achieve the career they want. But that's not all. I believe the same thoughtful and in-depth approach to creating the career you want also applies to your life outside of work.

As Maya Angelou said, *"I've learned that making a 'living' is not the same thing as 'making a life.'"* I want you to live your best life, both professionally and personally. I want to help you unlock your greatest potential and achieve the dreams you desire and deserve. To feel the fear and dive in anyway.

As a business leader, I have coached and mentored people to achieve outstanding results and success in their careers and personal lives through a set of four powerful strategies and approaches. I call it the D.E.E.P. process:

1. Design
2. Experience
3. Execute
4. Persevere

The D.E.E.P. process mirrors the artistic and physical execution of competitive divers. Skilled divers excel in the main elements of a dive score—their starting position/ approach (how they design their dive), their takeoff from the springboard (where their experience comes into play), their flight (how they execute their dive), and their rip entry (make the perfect splash and lasting impression). These areas align with how I want you to think about your life and career. Your starting position is your foundation and building blocks. You need to approach your dive to set yourself up for success. You need to leverage the springboard so you can take flight and fly. Ultimately, you must make a rip entry and a lasting impression. It takes effort, hard work, training, dedication, commitment, skill, and a ton of perseverance.

Belly Flops Happen

Skilled divers make it look graceful and effortless—but we all know it's not. The same is true in life. Sometimes we move through life effortlessly. But other times, we face barriers or obstacles. Though I have achieved much success, I've also experienced tough times, failures, tragedy, and personal hardships in my life. I've endured the loss of loved ones and tragic world events that impacted my family directly. I've experienced rejection, job changes, and, unfortunately, failed marriages. I refer to these instances as "belly flops." Some are more painful than others. Throughout these difficulties and belly flops, I've found comfort and resilience in the D.E.E.P. process, which I've used to get back on track and build a better life for myself and my family.

The goal here is to propel your life and career forward to achieve your deepest aspirations and reach personal satisfaction. But to achieve great results, you must dive into the process and dive into yourself deeply. In each chapter, I will share stories, advice, and some tips and tricks that will help you dive D.E.E.P. into YOU, your career, and your life goals. At the end of each chapter, I provide questions for you to reflect and plan accordingly.

I will share my journey as an ambitious, career-oriented woman who—despite the challenges of being a working mom (and then a single working mom)—went on to successfully juggle a career and personal life. Most of all, I will focus on the importance of confidence and self-belief, and how to leverage your strengths to advance your career and live the life you desire.

So, let's dive in.

STRATEGY 1

DESIGN:
YOUR APPROACH

TEST THE WATERS & FIND PURPOSE

"Twenty years from now you will be more disappointed by the things you didn't do than by the ones you did. So throw off the bowlines, sail away from the safe harbor. Catch the trade winds in your sails. Explore. Dream."
– Mark Twain

When I met John, he told me he struggled to get out of bed in the morning. After spending years in an unfulfilling but lucrative career, he had fallen into depression.

His dilemma was a difficult one: as boring as his job was, he was the main source of support for his family. Along with his wife and two children, he had just moved into a larger house, one that required every penny of his salary to maintain.

He couldn't see a way out.

"Joanie, I hate it," he confessed during our first phone call. "There's no point. I feel like a hamster running around in one of those wheels. I'm miserable at work, and I don't like the company I'm working for. I feel like I can't take it anymore. But we need the money."

His voice trailed off for a moment.

"I'm just not sure what else I could do for a living without taking a cut in pay. And we can't afford that," he continued.

As I listened to John, my empathy grew. His story wasn't unique. But to John—and to so many others trapped in unfulfilling careers—there seemed to be no way out.

"John, I'm sure there are more options out there than you probably realize," I said in my most soothing voice.

As our conversation continued, I learned more about John and his challenges. In his depressed state, nothing seemed solvable. While he had transferable skills, he also had few contacts outside of the financial services industry and little time and energy for an intensive job hunt.

It seemed clear to me that a lack of purpose had drained John's energy, leaving him vulnerable to depression and a state of hopelessness. Research backs up my thinking. A recent study by Gartner found that 52% of workers say the pandemic has made them question the purpose of their day-to-day job.[1] In the wake of the COVID-19 pandemic, nearly half of all employees surveyed were reconsidering their careers due to their desire to find more purpose in their lives.[2] In other words, employees whose careers lacked meaning were looking around for work that was more purposeful.

The Role of Passion in a Career

It seems like everyone has an opinion regarding the role passion plays in one's career. For some, a career without passion is meaningless. For others, work is a means to an end, and they seek purpose in their families, outside interests, or hobbies. Every generation that enters the workforce grapples with the same questions:

- Can I truly find a job or career that aligns with my interests?

- Can I find a career that will fulfill my dreams and aspirations?
- Can I make a living doing something I'm passionate about?

Believe me, John was far from the first individual I've coached who sought a mid-career reinvention. In fact, the search for purpose isn't confined to any specific career stage, age, generation, or occupation—anyone can grow discontented and seek new horizons or a renewed sense of purpose. Throughout my career, I've encountered many people who have found themselves stuck, unhappy, and depressed with the work they do every day. I have seen how a sense of purpose is fundamental to finding career satisfaction and fulfillment, while a lack of purpose creates a gap at work that is difficult to fill. After helping thousands of employees find work that fulfills their need for meaning, I've realized the key to finding purposeful work involves combining your values with work that makes a difference.

Increasingly, employees' desire for meaning at work is aligning with organizations that seek to enhance results and employee, stakeholder, and customer engagement through mission-driven products, services, and businesses. As Deloitte puts it: "Today's workers seek to identify with an organization's purpose, longing to connect at a deeper level to align their personal wants and desires with the organization's mission."[3]

Research conducted at Harvard Business School reveals that employees with a sense of purpose demonstrate increased job satisfaction and performance, which can lead to an increased sense of well-being, happiness, and better health.[4] Specifically, the benefits of a purpose-filled career include:[5]

- **Improved job satisfaction:** On average, researchers documented 13 percent higher job satisfaction for employees with work experience that incorporated social purpose over those who didn't have that type of focus.
- **Enhanced job performance:** A different study revealed that employees with social purpose were 24 percent more efficient and demonstrated 43 percent less downtime with no loss in quality compared to those who lacked such a purpose.
- **Enriched career prospects:** Employees with a sense of purpose at work—also known as job purposing—were 10 percent more likely to receive a raise and 40 percent more likely to gain a promotion.
- **Increased well-being:** Pursuing social purposes not only lowers the negative health effects of stress, but it also reduces stress responses at a cellular level. Social-purpose activities activate the pleasure-producing parts of the brain. These activities also lower cholesterol and blood pressure in groups of people performing acts of social purpose versus those without such purpose.

If you're still not convinced, I've got one final piece of evidence for you—a study by LinkedIn revealed that 49 percent of employees would trade part of their salary to add more purpose to their current role.[6] Not only that, but purpose-driven employees are also 30 percent more likely to demonstrate high performance and twice as likely to positively promote their employer without prompting.[7]

Turning Vision into Reality

While it's clear that many employees seek purpose-driven work, what is less clear is exactly how to achieve it. A sense of purpose is highly individual—what works for one person may not work for someone else.

The research I've just cited can help establish some ground rules for finding purpose at work. In my experience, understanding your own values and how you derive a sense of purpose is the first place to start. Then, once you've figured that out, determine whether your values and sense of purpose align with an organization's mission and values.

Maybe you're one of those people with a clear sense of your values. If so, that's great! Or maybe you're not exactly sure where you fall on the values spectrum. Regardless, you might want to take the Barrett Values Center Assessment, https://www.valuescentre.com/tools-assessments/pva/, which helps you determine what matters the most to you.[8] Values range from honesty, trust, and accountability to kindness, empathy, dedication, and environmental sensitivity.

Once you have a clear understanding of your own values, you will also have a much easier time deciding if a given role in a specific organization will help fulfill your sense of purpose. There are many online and free resources available to help you determine your strengths and values. If you are struggling to figure this out, it is worth the time to take a few assessments.

The second part of this process requires you to decide whether you can forge personal connection with an organization's mission and values. If you can't connect with a company's mission and values, that can—and probably should—be a dealbreaker. The best ways to determine if you and a company are a good fit involve digging into their mission and values.

Start with a company's stated mission and values, which are usually located in the "About Us" section of their website. But don't stop there—you don't want to take on a role only to find that the wonderful values on the company's website were mere lip service. To learn more, look at company job postings, the profiles of key executives, social media posts, and the latest news/events/comments/reviews from employees and former employees on sites like Glassdoor.

A word of caution: It is possible to conduct a thorough due diligence and still end up feeling disappointed with your role and your employer. In that situation, your job is to determine whether this disappointment or disaffection is temporary or permanent. If you're working on a challenging project or have a difficult co-worker, it can be easy to blame your role and/or your employer. However, challenging projects and difficult co-workers are part of virtually all job situations. They can be overcome with hard work and the right attitude.

Judging from my conversation with John, it seemed to me that his situation was a more permanent disaffection rather than a temporary disappointment. John didn't like his employer, a large nationwide financial institution. This company's reputation had taken a hit during the financial crisis, and John felt that the company lacked respect for both its customers and employees.

Not only that, but John also wondered if he had chosen the wrong career. Despite years of success in the accounting industry, he wondered if the career he had chosen more than a decade ago in college was responsible for his unhappiness at work. Like so many others, John was feeling trapped by a career decision made in his early 20s.

This dislike of his employer, boredom with his role, and uncertainty about his chosen career path placed John in a highly tenuous position. Lost and uncertain where to turn, he questioned if he could even make a change at this point in his life.

"Can I change careers?" he asked me during a later conversation. "What if I just can't do it?"

"John, it is never too late," I firmly reassured him. "I can help you make a plan and decide on the right path for success."

Finding the Right Path

To help him uncover his ideal path, I emailed John five questions that we would discuss the following week:

1. What classes did you enjoy in high school/college/ grad school and which ones did you excel in?
2. How would your friends and family describe your personality and what would they say your strengths and weaknesses are?
3. What do you like and dislike about your current job and career?
4. If money wasn't a factor, what type of work would you do?
5. How do you want to make a difference in this world?

For the first question, I wanted to know what studies and subjects interested John and the subjects that generated his best performance. Some people are gifted in math or science, while others are in English or the arts. I believe we all have different talents and gifts that we should leverage and play to our strengths. I wanted John to think back to his school days and remember the classes and work he enjoyed the most. What had come the easiest to him?

The second question is one I ask everyone I interview. Instead of asking someone what they think their strengths and weaknesses are, I like to ask someone what their *family or friends* would say their strengths and weaknesses are. In an interview, I phrase the question as if I were checking references on them. By doing this, most people will tell the truth about their strengths and weaknesses.

More importantly, our friends and family sometimes know us better than we know ourselves. They frequently offer valuable insights and opinions. In this case, I wanted John to think about what his friends and family would say. I hoped this question would prompt him to ask for input.

No matter what your role is, there will always be tasks that you enjoy and others you don't. For example, I love to work with people, and I enjoy talking to my team and customers daily. However, I don't love reading or reviewing legal contracts with pages of details. Regardless, in my position, I am required to do both well. I need to be a leader who possesses strong communication skills, and I have a fiduciary responsibility to my company to protect them and not sign a contract that would put us in a bad financial situation. Jobs are work. They take effort, commitment, and dedication. They require the completion of a variety of tasks. I asked John the third question because I wanted to know what work he enjoys doing and what work is tedious or boring to him.

The fourth question is a bit of a dreamer question. You might even say it is unrealistic. However, I like to ask this question to get to the heart of what John would truly love to do with his life. Let's say John didn't have to worry about supporting his family and paying a big, fat mortgage. In that case, what type of work would he want to do? This isn't a question about retiring or sitting on a beach sipping a cocktail. This question is meant to elicit clarity about what role John would choose in an ideal world. Interestingly, John shared that he briefly considered becoming a teacher.

However, his parents reacted in horror to that idea. They even discussed cutting off further support towards his college tuition and other expenses. John feared he wouldn't be able to earn a decent living as a teacher, so he chose accounting.

This question is also meaningful because it helps you—and me, the career counselor and recruiter—get to the foundation of what type of work you find most rewarding. With that knowledge in hand, it's easier to build a career path that achieves personal and professional alignment while still making a decent living.

The last question involves legacy and impact. John needed to understand what was most important to him and how he wanted to make an impact. What would he like his legacy to be? This question also aligns with values and can tell me if someone is more concerned with making a lot of money or the happiness of their family. There is no right or wrong answer, but the answer should be about what is most important to *you*. What difference do you want to make? What do you care about? I had a good friend who was a firefighter. He knew he would never be wealthy from being a firefighter, but he was passionate about fighting fires and saving lives. He was clear about his passion and desire to make a difference, and he loved what he did.

Your legacy and values will also evolve as you mature and gain different experiences. The key to answering this question involves doing work that you care about and that matters to you. John was suffering in his role because he didn't believe he was making a difference or a positive contribution to his company and the people around him. How John—or you—defines legacy or worth is highly individual. Whether you're a waitress bringing a cup of coffee to a customer, a doctor saving a life, or an IT engineer designing new state-of-the-art cyber technology—what matters is not so much the task or the role, but the meaning that you derive from it. These examples all make a difference in someone's world.

When you're young, choosing a career and profession can be overwhelming or incredibly easy (often, it's the former). You might have known since you were a small child that you wanted to be a doctor, a scientist, a veterinarian, or a teacher. Or maybe you had no clue where to turn. As your career evolves, you may experience multiple careers or roles. In fact, the U.S. Bureau of Labor Statistics states that the average number of jobs during a career is 12.[9]

When I was attending college, I decided to get a part-time job at a local florist. The owner of the shop was eager for me to do more than just answer the phones, take orders, and work at the register. He let me start experimenting with making floral arrangements, which I picked up rather quickly. I had always loved flowers and was interested in learning more. I became quite good at making the floral arrangements, and it was fun to work on weddings, celebrations, and special events.

But there was also another side to the business—funerals. I had a hard time with the funerals. It was difficult taking the orders for funeral arrangements and talking to a very upset person on the other end of the phone, who would often share a story about their deceased loved one. I tried to listen, be comforting, and send my condolences, but it was weighing on me. The worst part was receiving a call about a child's funeral. I took all the stories to heart, and eventually I realized I had a hard time dealing with all the death I was exposed to. Even though I didn't know the deceased, I would take their stories home with me. The sadness of the customers stayed with me. I realized that my part-time job, which was supposed to be wonderful and filled with beauty, had another side to it that was sad and dark. I knew this wouldn't be a field I would want to stay in or work in that long. Sometimes we need these experiences to figure out what we want and don't want to do. I decided to give notice, and I determined a career dealing with death or end of life services wasn't something I would ever be good at.

Early Influences Can Guide You

When my children were younger, I exposed them to different hobbies, sports, and performing arts. I wasn't sure where their interests or strengths would lie, but I wanted them to try different things at an early age so they could figure out what they loved to do and what they were good at. Both my son and daughter participated in soccer, sailing, tennis, and swim team together. My son also played t-ball, baseball, basketball, football, and golf. My daughter took piano and singing lessons, art class, horseback riding, and dance. They were active, busy kids during their early childhood and elementary years. I was also exhausted and broke trying to keep up with it all, but it was fun and a true joy for me.

As they entered middle school, they both found activities they were passionate about and talented in. Chase, my son, focused on golf. He made the high school golf team while he was still in middle school. He played golf all through high school, and his team even made it to the State Championships twice while he was there. He played in tournaments outside school and attended camps during the summer. As I write this book, my son is attending college and is enrolled in a PGA Golf Management program. So far, he is loving his major and excited about his future career in the golf field. Time will tell if he stays with this as a career choice, but I have tried to encourage him to pursue a career field that he is interested in and passionate about.

My daughter, Ashley, is in her senior year of high school. I call her my dancing scientist. She spent her middle school and high school years on multiple competition dance teams. She is a member of the National Honors Society and will graduate with a double HS diploma, including one from the fine arts program. Ashley loves art and science, and she's infatuated with watching *Grey's Anatomy*. She is involved in the pre-med club, student government, and volunteers at a local hospital. I'm not sure what she will choose to study in college, but she has developed great foundations and experiences to leverage in whatever she decides to do. My hope is that she ends up in a career and field she loves and is passionate about.

I have always loved the saying: "Choose a job you love, and you will never work a day in your life." I believe there is truth to these words. If you find a job that you enjoy and have an opportunity to make a difference, it is much easier to put in the effort, dedication, and hard work to be successful. On the other hand, life isn't a bowl of cherries. There will be plenty of ups and downs, twists, and turns throughout your career. You may end up doing a few somersaults or experience some belly flops, but that is okay. Work is a lot easier when you love or at least like what you do. Try to find a field that inspires you and interests you.

When Interests and Careers Align

You may be fortunate in that a personal interest or hobby led you to a long-lasting, rewarding career. Or you may have fallen randomly into a satisfying career that you never expected. I can assure you that you—and everyone else who is employed—are on your own journey and will find your own path. While it isn't always easy, it is possible for you to find a satisfying career that will pay your bills. Work won't always be fun, but at one point or another, you will likely find it challenging, demanding, stressful, tedious, rewarding, fulfilling, and joyful.

I enjoy hearing stories of people who have started their businesses because they're pursuing their passion or interests. Sometimes it comes from an idea they must create, or from them inventing a product to make their lives or lives of others better. One of my favorites is the story of how Sara Blakely, the founder of SPANX, was getting ready for a party and realized she didn't have the right undergarment to provide a smooth look under white pants.[10] She took scissors to a pair of control top pantyhose and cut the legs off. Her idea was brilliant, and in 2000, she started her company. It has since become a whole new industry and changed the world of female undergarments and clothing.[11]

You've probably heard other stories of entrepreneurs filling a need—Debi Fields of Mrs. Fields Cookies, or Mark Zuckerberg, who started Facebook as a college project. At the beginning of these endeavors, the entrepreneur or inventor may have little or no idea of the impact they're going to have on the world. They all had to work hard and put in the effort, dedication, and creativity necessary. And they had roadblocks and obstacles they overcame. They dealt with rejection, had to obtain investors, and put in a lot of sweat equity to make it happen. Career success is not easy, but it can happen if you align your passion, seek to make a difference in the world, and put in the effort and work required. The truth is that you, John, or any other individual possesses the ability to create or invent something new.

Making the Reverse Twist

During the next few months, John and I talked more about the answers to his questions. We discussed how he might find a path that would provide a sense of purpose and meet his needs for a specific level of income. I coached John to the realization that he did enjoy accounting—what he disliked was the industry he worked in and the specific company that employed him.

The environment wasn't the right fit for John. He didn't feel motivated or energized to do the work. So, he decided to start a search for a new job—still in accounting, but in a different industry that would be more rewarding. John realized that it was important he work for a company that aligned with his personal values. Realizing what he needed, he was able to overcome his depression and take some concrete steps towards changing careers. John began to network, and it wasn't long before a leadership opportunity arose in the education industry.

Ultimately, John accepted a role as the head of finance at a prestigious Northeast private school. His new job came with the opportunity to serve as an accounting adjunct professor at a local college. Both John and I were thrilled—his ability to find a job using his skills, at a competitive level of pay, in an industry that aligned with his values, was a literal dream come true.

Your job may not always provide complete satisfaction. There will be twists and turns on your career path. Paths are not linear—careers bring surprises, and there will be opportunities to learn and try new things. It is important to take the good experiences *and* learn from the bad ones.

After years of experience in recruitment and navigating my own career, I can share that there are many options, choices, and opportunities for all of us. You may feel like you have thrown yourself into the deep end of the pool. Perhaps it feels uncomfortable being there. Don't panic. If you find yourself in a position of treading water or even feel like you may be drowning, you can swim to the side of the pool and rest. It's okay to pause and reevaluate or alter your strategy. Sometimes you will need to test the waters. You may need to try different fields, different companies, or a different boss. All of this is okay—just make sure you take your time and follow the D.E.E.P. process.

CHAPTER ONE REFLECTION

Ideally, you want your personal core values to align with those of your employer and/or career path, so that you find greater meaning and purpose in your career and life. Take the time to examine and explore your core personal values.

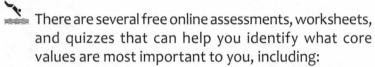 There are several free online assessments, worksheets, and quizzes that can help you identify what core values are most important to you, including:
- Brene Brown, Author, *Dare to Lead*, List of Values https://brenebrown.com/resources/dare-to-lead-list-of-values/
- Gyfted website, Personal Value Assessment https://www.gyfted.me/quiz-landing/values-assessment
- Barrett Values Center Assessment https://www.valuescentre.com/tools-assessments/pva/

Narrow your core values down to your top 5, then explore what you've learned.

What classes did you enjoy in high school/college/grad school and which ones did you excel in?

What do you like and dislike about your current job and career?

How would your friends and family describe your personality and what would they say your strengths and weaknesses are?

If money wasn't a factor, what type of work would you do?

How do you want to make an impact? What would you like your legacy to be?

MY STARTING BLOCKS

"I am not afraid … I was born to do this."
– Joan of Arc

Before I go too "deep" on further career advice, I want to share a bit about my personal upbringing and provide some additional context. Childhood establishes our values system and provides us multiple life-lessons. Looking back on my childhood, I didn't know exactly what my future had in store. I can't say I visualized that one day I would be an executive in the business world. But what I do remember is my parents' constant encouragement to put in the effort to accomplish my goals, and their advice that doing so would lay the foundation for my successes in life. From the outside, I wasn't anything special—just a girl from Queens with a hard-working middle-class family who loved, supported, and believed in her. My family provided a safe space to dream and aspire, and the encouragement and confidence to pursue my dreams. Whether I was singing a solo in the school chorus, acting in the school play, trying out for the dance team, or running for student government, I went for it because I was encouraged and supported to pursue my desires.

Here's some insight into my starting blocks in life.

My parents met on a summer day in 1965. They married nearly five years later, and I came along just shy of their first-year wedding anniversary. Though my parents didn't come from great riches and fortune, they did provide my three sisters and me the most generous gifts in life. The three gifts are:

1. Unconditional love
2. Strong work ethic
3. Confidence

I view these gifts as my foundation and starting blocks in life. I was fortunate to receive them from both my parents and grandparents. While they aren't always available to everyone, these gifts are within all of us—right at our fingertips. I wish they would be shared more equally throughout society. My hope is that I can pass them on to my children, family, friends, colleagues, and to you.

My Father's Work Ethic

I was five years old when I first experienced the uncertainty of the job market. My dad, an electrician, was laid off in 1976 during the middle of the energy crisis. Rising inflation, a recession, and the aftereffects of the Vietnam War and Watergate had created a society and economy in turmoil.[12]

Like millions of other Americans, my dad was caught in a recession that resulted in 7.8 percent inflation in 1976.[13] Although I wasn't aware of all the challenges that resulted from unemployment, I do remember that my mom went back to work as an emergency room nurse, while dad took over homemaking duties. A few times I went to school with uneven pigtails, but I recognized he had his hands full taking care of my sisters and me.

My family didn't have much money for extra luxuries or fancy vacations. My dad's unemployment meant we faced financial hardships. I remember my mom using food stamps to pay for our groceries. I asked her what they were and where she got them. She explained that it was a government benefit since dad was out of work.

We lived in a small two-bedroom attached home in Fresh Meadows, Queens. We had our fair share of obstacles, including four girls living in one small bedroom. As years passed and both parents were hard at work, we moved into larger homes, and I ended up attending a private grammar school. It was still challenging for them to provide that education, but they made it a priority.

Though the late 1970s were probably one of the most challenging times for our family, fortunately, my dad wasn't unemployed for long. As an electrician with the International Brotherhood of Electrical Workers (IBEW), Local 3 union, he enjoyed a rewarding career, working all around New York City, especially in the World Trade Center. One of the highlights of his career involved installing the antenna on top of the World Trade Center.

Trips to the World Trade Center were regular highlights of my childhood. One day, when my cousins from Massachusetts were visiting, I had the experience of a lifetime. It remains a very special day from my childhood.

"Joanie," my dad said. "Do you want to climb up into the antenna?"

"Really, dad? Could I?" I replied, jumping up and down. I'd never imagined something so exciting.

As we climbed up the stairs inside of the North Tower's antenna, I noticed thousands of cable lines running up and down the walls. At that time, *this* was the most powerful high frequency antenna in the United States.

"See that door over there, Joanie?" my dad asked. "That door allows me and my friends to climb outside on the antenna to get to the top and change the lightbulbs out there. I was one of the first guys to go up there and change those bulbs."

"Really? Wow!" I was super impressed.

My dad was also involved in electricity projects at the Empire State Building. In fact, he was one of the electricians who changed the lightbulb at the very tip-top of the building. One day, he allowed me to bring one of the old foot-long light bulbs from the top of the Empire State building to school for Show-and-Tell.

Imagine trusting an elementary school kid with a foot-long, fragile light bulb? But he did. And my classmates—and teacher—were thrilled. I was the proudest kid in class as I shared that my father, my superhero, had climbed to the top of the Empire State Building to change the light bulb that lit up New York City.

My dad started in the trades as an apprentice. He followed in his father's and older brothers' footsteps, working his way to become an electrician. He took on stretch assignments and was never afraid of putting in the extra effort and hard work required to be successful. My dad took on challenging assignments to learn new things, make more money, and advance his career. Eventually, he moved into leadership roles, built a strong reputation in his industry, and became admired in his field. My dad's story is a great example of how a hardworking and dedicated employee can advance their career, find balance, and live a wonderful life.

My father's employment journey also led him to a very successful role as a project manager for Morgan Stanley through IBEW Local 3. He traded his blue-collar shirts for button downs and slacks and began overseeing the electric for the trading floors at Morgan Stanley. This career opportunity brought him back to the World Trade Center. As you can imagine, it later caused much sorrow and grief for him. He was there during the bombing in 1993 and the terrorist attack on September 11. He was extremely fortunate to escape from the 54th floor of the South Tower on that dreadful day—a day none of us will ever forget.

I remember receiving a voicemail that morning from my mother. She said, "Joanie, I wanted to let you know dad called and left a message that a plane hit the World Trade Center. But it was the other tower, and he's okay." I remember thinking it was probably a small Cessna that may have hit the antenna. But then my sister called and told me to turn on the TV. I was living on Long Island at the time, just a few blocks away from my parents' home. After seeing the news, I jumped in my car and raced to be with my mom.

She sat on the couch watching the TV in disbelief and horror. Complete anguish overcame us. We knew that dad was in the South Tower. As we watched the two towers burning, one by one my sisters arrived at my parents' house. At 9:59 a.m., we watched in terror as the South Tower collapsed. We had not heard from my father, and I feared the worst.

I'm not sure how much time went by. It seemed like an eternity. Finally, the phone rang, and my mother answered. I will never forget her cracking voice as she screamed, "Charrrrllllieeee?" She could hardly get his name out, but it was him. My dad had walked down 54 flights in the South Tower and was a few blocks away from the site when it collapsed. My mom handed me the phone. I had to hear his voice for myself.

"Dad, are you really out?" I asked. "The tower collapsed. Are you really out? You aren't just calling to say goodbye, right?"

"Joanie, I am really out," he replied. "I'm okay. I don't have a scratch on me."

I wanted to believe him, but I was terrified of what I was watching on television. He said he was going to walk to the Brooklyn Bridge and get a ride home. About 20 minutes later, he called back and said, "I want you girls to know I am okay. I got out."

My family and I are eternally thankful that he escaped and made it home to us that evening.

Unfortunately—like so many others—my dad lost many friends, colleagues, and his best friend since third grade, Glenn J. Travers. Glenn was the best man at my parents' wedding, and to my family he was Uncle Glenn. Like the tens of thousands of Americans who survived those attacks, my dad was changed forever.

A few years after the 9/11 attacks, he decided to retire. Working in Manhattan where he'd been for so long, in a landscape forever changed by the destruction of the Twin Towers, was too difficult. My mom, sisters, and I were grateful for his decision.

My dad's career story exemplifies the twists and turns that a career can take over the course of 30 or 40 years. Throughout my life, my dad's confidence and belief in himself and his skills inspired me, my mom, and my sisters to go out into the world and make a difference.

Mom Wore the Pants

You may be surprised after all the bragging I've done about my dad to learn that *my mom* was the one who wore the pants in the family. There was no doubt from my sisters and me: my mother ruled the roost and laid down the law in our home. Born to a large Irish Catholic family, my mom was the eighth of nine children. When she shares her stories of childhood, I'm sad to hear that she wasn't given the attention, love, and support that my sisters and I received.

Ever since I was little, my mom has been one of the smartest people I've ever known. She is the type of person who knows every answer on *Jeopardy!*, but she would never brag about that. While she did well from an educational standpoint—taking advanced and honors classes all through high school—my mom didn't receive any recognition or attention for her accomplishments, except from her oldest sister, Eileen. To this day, my mom cherishes the kindness and recognition her sister gave her. Looking back, her parents—my grandparents—were likely too preoccupied with providing for their large family to give my mom the praise and recognition she so deserved.

When my mother would come home from school with straight A's, my grandparents would say, "Wow, you're still in the honors classes?" The choice of their words impacted her confidence at an early age. My mother grew up in a home where the boys received more of the attention and could do no wrong.

Not only did my mother successfully raise four daughters and run a household, but she decided to go back to school and become a nurse when my sister Diana and I were little. She even stayed in nursing school when she became pregnant with my twin sisters. Luckily, her teachers and professors encouraged her to finish her education, even while expecting twins. She went on to complete her bachelor's and master's in psychiatric nursing—with a 4.0 GPA all the way through grad school.

I was a proud teenager when my mom graduated Magna Cum Laude from Adelphi University. A true learner, she could have gone on to get a PhD if she hadn't been too busy working as a nurse. She recalls that she was probably smarter than most doctors in her early days working as a nurse. But she now realizes that she lacked confidence. Despite her academic accomplishments, she wasn't raised to think or believe that she could do or be anything. I guess that is why she made it her mission to support and encourage all four of her daughters.

My mom was a fantastic role model, setting an incredible example of how to successfully balance getting an education, having a career, and raising four girls. With my dad supporting and encouraging her along the way, she was able to change the narrative for herself—and my sisters and me – through her drive, ambition, and unwavering work ethic.

Aside from being a hard-working professional and a devoted parent, my mom also volunteered her time to help others. Despite our challenges, she realized how fortunate our family was. She would make meals and deliver them to the sick and elderly through the Meals on Wheels program. We lived in a close-knit neighborhood, and our friends always knew they could count on my mom—whether that meant mentoring young babysitters or taking time to have a cup of tea with the lonely old widower down the street. Her caring nature and her ability to listen to and empathize with others no doubt led her to choose the challenging field of psychiatric nursing. Her influence undoubtedly planted the seeds in me to support and advise others to achieve the best in life.

I hit the jackpot with both my parents and am so grateful for the foundation they provided me. They also provided me with three built-in best friends (sisters) that I adore.

Girls, Girls Everywhere: My Extended Family

My sisters and I always felt bad that my dad didn't have a son to play sports with. But at the same time, he would always dismiss those concerns and say girls were the best. So instead, we all learned to fish and know a thing or two about the New York Mets. The four of us were proud to be women, and we never felt inferior to men. We were raised to believe men and women were created equally, with equal potential to succeed. The confidence my parents and extended family instilled in me helped me succeed as a strong woman and pass that belief onto my children.

Sometimes I wonder if our situation would have changed if a brother had been added to the equation. Would I be different? Would that have changed how I saw myself? It certainly would have changed the family dynamic, but I also believe that my mother would have made sure we all were supported and treated equally. However, being the oldest of an all-girl family—and the fact that I was raised to believe we could do or achieve anything we set our minds to—made me into the person I am today. My parents would say, "You are a Bily. You can do anything!" We felt like we had superpowers. In some ways, we were made to feel we were better than boys.

My sisters and I loved visiting my dad's father. On weekends, grandpa's house was full of my aunts, uncles, and their kids. Ironically, all my cousins from my dad's side of the family who lived on Long Island were girls: my family of four girls, my uncle's three girls, and my aunt's two girls. All together there were nine girls running around. Let me tell you, we had a blast working on productions, which we believed to be worthy of Broadway.

We all believed our families were getting together just to watch us perform some magical dance routine or singing number that was sure to be picked up by the next Broadway director. Of course, we had disagreements and arguments over who was the star and who would sing the main number. Sometimes an aunt would have to intervene and find some peace amongst nine bossy girls. But all in all, we had fun. The night always ended with my grandfather singing *Thank Heaven for Little Girls* on his player piano. We would all gather around the piano and listen to his loud and pure belting.

When I was very young, my parents didn't have the extra money to send me to a dance studio and buy me all the shoes and leotards that were required. Fortunately, I did have somewhat of a Fairy Godmother moment. A very special aunt of mine observed that I didn't have the leotards or dance shoes that my cousins had. My aunt Mary Royce, also known as Muffin Mary (I'll explain later) lived in Framingham, Massachusetts, with her husband Bob and their three sons. Everyone in the family loved Muffin Mary because she was full of life, laughter, and fun. Although we only saw the Royce family a few times a year, we all looked forward to their visits, which usually ended up with Muffin Mary dancing on tables—no joke!

Once Aunt Mary noticed my lack of dance supplies, she whisked me off to the local dance store and began outfitting me with all the latest Capezio tap shoes and ballet attire. I literally felt like Cinderella with my Fairy Godmother. She flew around the store, grabbing me a leotard, ballet shoes, tights, a light pink wraparound ballet skirt, and a dance bag to carry it all around in. What a magical day! I look back and remember that as one of the best days of my life. How fortunate I was to have an aunt who showed me such generosity and kindness.

Growing up, it was always fun to learn what Muffin Mary was up to next. She started her own modeling agency in Boston when my cousins were younger. After that, she went on to learn belly dancing, and eventually she fell in love with Arabian horses, even competing in and winning dressage competitions. Before long, she started breeding her horses, a love that she and her husband Bob shared. Aunt Mary always pursued her desires, thoughts, and dreams. And there is no doubt she had fun doing all those things. She was a fabulous role model to me at a very young age. She now lives on the Cape and—while she enjoys time with her grandkids—she is still going strong in her 80s. In fact, she recently started taking guitar lessons—a true testament to her drive, curiosity, and commitment to lifelong learning.

I would be remiss not to mention how my famous Aunt Mary got her nickname. You might remember I mentioned growing up in an Irish Catholic family. Well, both of my parents had sisters named Mary. Then I also had uncles who married Marys, and many of my aunts named their daughters Mary. Needless to say, we had a lot of "Marys" running around. So, when I was little, I decided to call this Aunt Mary "Muffin Mary" because she had a dog named Muffin. The name stuck. I still call her that today.

I'd like to believe we all have a bit of Muffin Mary in us. Not only her love of living life to the fullest and pursuing her dreams, but more importantly her observant, generous, and kind nature. Her generosity and kindness specifically gave me a boost of confidence at a very early age. She made me feel special and loved, and for that I am eternally grateful. I also learned from her a valuable lesson: the importance of making others feel special and cared for.

So now you know quite a bit about my starting blocks—love, demonstrated work ethic, kindness, and confidence. This was my foundation in life, and I am grateful for every bit of it. The good and the bad, the ups and the downs. I don't take any of it for granted. It all propels me to keep working hard, moving forward, and reaching for my dreams. I believe the foundations of work ethic, support, encouragement, love, kindness, and confidence, make a difference in people's lives. I pledge to pass these gifts onto others. Let's make them contagious!

CHAPTER TWO REFLECTION

Your unique life journey and experiences guide your career choices and shape your everyday interactions with the world. Your upbringing and influences are points on your life map. These points tell you how to navigate every experience and tend to play a role in your life and career choices. Let's explore YOU.

Everyone has their own unique story; what's yours? What makes you, you?

What foundational starting blocks have you formed early in your life?

What challenges have you overcome that have made you stronger?

How can you use those challenges or hardships in your life to your advantage?

How can you share the great gifts of unconditional love, a strong work ethic, and building confidence in others?

PREDICT YOUR FUTURE

"The best way to predict the future is to create it."
– Abraham Lincoln

With Career Day on the horizon at my children's middle school a few years ago, their principal asked me to participate as a guest speaker. Parents who were lawyers, firefighters, nurses, and doctors came in and answered questions about their careers. My role, in contrast, was to discuss the most popular careers and the types of work that were emerging for employers and employees in the future.

I looked forward to the day, but I must be honest— speaking to a group of middle school students can be more intimidating than being live on national TV. Teenagers can be a tough audience, especially my own kids, who weren't exactly thrilled at the prospect of me potentially embarrassing them while I was on stage.

"Mom, what are you going to tell the students?" Chase asked me.

"I thought I would discuss what new careers are emerging and talk about some of the fastest growing jobs that are in demand," I replied.

"Mom, what is it that you do, exactly?" he asked. "It's hard for me to explain to my friends what you do because I'm not sure myself. When they ask, I just say, 'She's on TV,' but I know that's not the right answer."

I smiled.

"Chase, I help people find great jobs," I said. "And I help companies find great people to hire. Sometimes, that means helping someone find their first job. Other times, it may involve helping someone get a new big role or promotion. I love what I do because it makes a difference in people's lives and hopefully allows them to live their best professional and personal life."

I love what I do. Every day brings new jobs and new challenges. That's why I've spent the last 25 years working in the employment industry. My role as a recruiting executive gives me visibility across the employment landscape in America and the changing operations of companies in virtually all industries.

My work has taken me to the front lines of industries across the country including:

- Corporate headquarters for many Fortune 500 companies
- Production floors of the automotive industry
- The trading floors of New York City's top brokerage firms
- Manufacturing plants of top food suppliers
- Surgical suites and intensive care units of hospitals
- State of the art distribution centers for the largest logistic companies in the world

What have I learned from these experiences? Well, I've had to assess the talent and skills these organizations need to run efficiently and effectively. To help shape the future of employment, I must be on the front lines, acting as a partner in the growth strategies of companies large and small. To grow and thrive, organizations need the best talent available. Helping them meet that need is my job.

The Forces Shaping Employment

Automation will cost 45 million Americans their jobs by 2030, the McKinsey Global Institute predicted in February 2021.[14] Disruptions caused by COVID-19 have sped up the pace of automation, rapidly transforming how the world works in both the goods production and service sectors.

Just look at what happened to the travel agent industry even before the onset of COVID. Competitive online sites put many travel agents out of business. During the last decade, many occupations have declined, including travel agents, data entry keyers, word processors and typists, parking enforcement workers, and switchboard operators (the U.S. Bureau of Labor Statistics lists these as the fastest declining occupations).[15]

The destruction of jobs from automation doesn't spell the end of healthy employment in America—far from it. In fact, employment is projected to grow. While millions of jobs will be lost to automation, millions of *other* jobs will be created. Overall, employment in the United States is projected to grow by 6 million jobs between 2019 and 2029, from 162.8 million to 168.8 million.

For my talk on Career Day to the middle school students, I drew on a recent speech I had given to my work colleagues on talent disruption. I discussed how advancements in technology, artificial intelligence, and automation are rapidly transforming the landscape of work. Many occupations are being eliminated or replaced with robotics and machines. This phenomenon is nothing new. We have seen frequent transformation and creative destruction over the last century.

In simple terms, this long-held theory states that economic structures are incessantly destroyed and reinvented. Just think of horse-drawn carriages being replaced by the locomotive, then automobiles and airlines. You probably remember how Blockbuster was replaced by Netflix. Think about having to get in your car, drive to a store, choose DVDs, pay to rent them, go back home, watch them, and then return them to the store before they're overdue. The whole process seems incredibly time-consuming now when you can just go on any device and play movies through Netflix, Hulu, Disney Plus, or Prime Video. Today you can instantly watch whatever you want.

Blockbuster is no longer around due to this economic concept called "creative destruction." Successful innovation is normally a source of temporary market power, eroding the profits and position of old firms that ultimately succumb to the pressure of new inventions commercialized by competing entrants. However, there's more to this story. Blockbuster passed up a chance in 2000 to purchase Netflix for $50 million.[16]

Clearly, Blockbuster's decision not to purchase Netflix when it had the chance represented a missed opportunity to adapt to the changes, or creative destruction, occurring within its industry. While creative destruction can—as in the case of video stores/streaming services—result in the destruction of entire industries, it can also result in the complete reinvention of companies and industries, which then changes the landscape of jobs and opportunities.

Today, there are many innovations disrupting and impacting the structure of America's labor force and every phase of the supply chain cycle. Nowadays, artificial intelligence can automatically sort, scan, and spot defects, robots weld parts on a manufacturing line, augmented reality devices increase plant productivity, and unmanned vehicles fetch products in warehouses and deliver them to workers for packaging.

This is our new reality. And it isn't going away. Automation and technological advances in manufacturing and production will continue to meet the demands of a consumer society in need of rapid fulfillment. Let's face it: we want a refrigerator that can order groceries for us when it's empty and drones that can deliver those groceries, right? Well, those wants are impacting and changing where the jobs of today and the future will be.

Adapting to a Changing Work Reality

I prepared for my presentation to the middle schoolers just as I would for any speech on employment and industry trends, regardless of the audience. Once I finalized my research and career trend information, I put together a few slides to share with the students. I also researched the latest government labor data, preparing to discuss the industries that were adding the most jobs and those that were experiencing the greatest decline.

According to the latest research from the Bureau of Labor Statistics, the total U.S. economy is projected to add 8.3 million jobs from 2021 - 2031, with employment reaching a level of 166.5 million. As of January 2023, there are 160 million employed workers in the U.S. and labor participation is only at 62.4%. Most of the job growth is forecasted in healthcare, professional and business services, state and local government, and the leisure and hospitality sectors. The emerging jobs will be in science, data mining and analysis, marketing analytics, digital transformation specialists, software developers, statisticians, and security and network engineers. The U.S. will continue to have a strong demand for registered nurses and physical therapists.

Another crucial point I planned to make was regarding the importance of education. I reflected in my presentation the direct correlation between education, employment, and higher lifetime earnings. In 2021, American workers with bachelor's degrees had an unemployment rate of 3.1% compared to an unemployment rate of 6.2% for those with only a high school diploma.[17]

My presentation included detailed information about growing industries. For instance, abundant opportunities will continue to exist in STEM—Science, Technology, Engineering, and Mathematics—industries. I can assure you these positions will continue to be in demand for years to come.

The Bureau of Labor Statistics predicts occupations in STEM will grow faster than any other profession. Jobs in STEM are projected to increase almost 11% by 2031, where non-STEM are projected to grow at 4.9%.

Aligning Skills with Jobs

The biggest challenge in the job market today is gaining the right skills, as they are rapidly changing. To learn about what skills are likely to be needed in the future, I researched information available at the McKinsey Global Institute on workforce skills and data from the World Economic Forum.

By viewing advancements in technology, robotics, and AI, we can see that the skills required in the workplace are changing. And so are the jobs. Based on the research I conducted, we see an evolving skill set will include a blend of soft skills and hard skills. There will be a higher need for digital and technical skills, plus higher cognitive, social, and emotional skills.

What I personally love about this research is that it refutes the theory that robots are completely taking over. Here's a list of the key skills needed for the future:[17][18]

- Critical thinking
- Complex problem-solving
- Social intelligence
- Adaptive thinking
- Creativity
- Negotiation
- Collaboration
- Emotional intelligence
- Cross-cultural competency
- Cognitive flexibility
- Empathy and communication
- Service orientation
- People management

Not only is automation continuing to disrupt the employment landscape, but the pandemic has also increased the pace of change. The World Economic Forum believes that as employers continue to adopt new technologies, 50 percent of all current employees will need new skills by 2025.[19] In fact, a study released in October 2022 by Amazon and Workplace Intelligence found that 70% of people don't feel prepared for the future of work. New skills that employers are identifying as useful include active learning, resilience, stress tolerance, and flexibility. Most employers expect their employees will pick up new skills on the job—much of it through online training.[20]

Of all the skills in demand, I would contend that the most important skill, by far, is the ability to learn. We must become lifelong learners. When anyone asks what the next "hot" skill will be, I tell them it's the same skill that has served people in the past and will continue to serve people today, tomorrow, and far into the future—the ability to learn and a commitment to continuous learning.

As technologies continue to evolve and business conditions shift, employees must stay in learning mode, so their skills don't lose currency. With the world moving as fast as it is, we must continue to be a society of people who are always learning new things. And as the importance of learning grows, the ways in which we learn will evolve too.

I was looking forward to the school assembly and was well prepared to share all this data with the children. As I took the stage in the school auditorium and saw the students, I suddenly thought: *How am I going to make this fun and engaging?* The principal introduced me to the students and shared that I was a regular guest speaker on the national news. That got their attention—for about 30 seconds.

At that moment, I had a realization about my audience and the best way to connect with them. I decided that I was going to ditch the opening of my presentation and instead ask the kids what they thought about the job market of the future. I asked them: What jobs will exist in the future that don't exist today? What jobs will be the best emerging jobs of the future? I was thrilled and astonished with their answers.

The students started calling out the various jobs they wanted in the future, including:

- Drone operator
- Video game creator
- Rocket pilot
- Space travel air traffic controller
- Robotic engineer
- Environmental engineer
- Virtual reality engineer

They asked me if I thought there would be jobs on Mars and what those jobs would be. I loved seeing the students' imaginations in full force and was thrilled to have them so engaged. Children know how to dream. It comes naturally to them. I also realized these kids were a great source of information and research. In fact, McKinsey, the World Economic Forum, and the Bureau of Labor Statistics may want to start a few research projects with middle schoolers. They know where technology is going before we do. They know how fast the world is changing, and they are on the front lines of the latest gaming technology.

My last piece of advice to the students was to make sure they have the chance to experience different careers and industries. I encouraged them to seize internships in college and gain experience in fields they are interested in. I encouraged them to learn from mentors and colleagues and to make long-lasting connections. I challenged them to take on stretch assignments and learning opportunities. We will discuss all of this and more in future chapters.

CHAPTER THREE REFLECTION

Now that you've examined your personal values, goals, and reviewed your starting blocks, it's time to discover what career paths align with those while also offering long-term growth potential. Start by researching and understanding the current and future employment landscape and trends to ensure long-term growth opportunities. Take the time to read articles and research reports about your interests.

Here are a few resources to get you started:

- https://www.bls.gov/careeroutlook/2022/home.htm
- U.S. Bureau of Labor Statistics' Occupational Outlook Handbook (https://www.bls.gov/ooh/)
- CareerOneStop (https://www.careeronestop.org/)

What fields and industries have the most growth potential for you?

How do your interests align with those growth industries?

Based on current trends, where do you see the most advancement and opportunity?

What volunteer opportunities are available in the field that interests you?

DREAM BIG

"If you can dream it, you can do it."
– Walt Disney

During the uncertainty of 2020, I joined a book club with fellow businesswomen, aiming to have a network of people to support and inspire each other. Some of the women I knew from the staffing industry, while others I had never met before. We had originally planned to get together in person to celebrate my good friend and mentor Joyce Russell's release of her book, *Put a Cherry on Top.* Unfortunately, we were not able to meet in person, so we got together on a video call to cheer on Joyce and hear about her book. We all enjoyed the connection so much that we decided to continue meeting once a month to support one another. Every month we shared stories, read, and discussed books, took virtual cooking lessons and virtual yoga, and did so much more. Just like that, our Lady Leaders Book Club was formed—one of the better things to come out of the pandemic.

Even more exciting was that the Lady Leaders decided to write a book together. *Together We Rise* is a collection of 15 stories from women in leadership on how we've stayed afloat, created opportunities, and established ourselves as powerful women in business. If you haven't read it yet, I encourage you to do so. These women are amazing leaders and accomplished executives. The best part about writing the book together is that I now have 14 women who have become close friends, cheerleaders, and supporters. They comprise the best network I have been a member of.

My chapter in the book *Together We Rise* is titled "Dream Big." Dreaming big is something I believe in and encourage others to do. I want people to live their best lives and fulfill their dreams and purpose. It is something I am passionate about, which is why I wanted to publish this book. I am including a version of my chapter from *Together We Rise* because my book and my story wouldn't be complete without it.

"Dream Big" (from *Together We Rise*)

Dream Big — How to Set Goals, Prioritize, and Achieve Your Aspirations

It was New Year's Eve, and I sat quietly by myself after putting my kids down to sleep. This would normally be a fun night out, or maybe a romantic dinner with a good bottle of wine while we watched the ball drop—but not this year. It was a quiet night, which I would spend thinking and reflecting on the past year and my plans for the future. It was normally an enjoyable time of self-reflection and planning for the new year. In the past, I've always enjoyed settings goals and having a few New Year's resolutions. This year was different.

I had just moved back to Long Island to be close to my parents and sisters after separating from my husband. My son, Chase, was about six at the time. My daughter, Ashley, was three. The kids and I moved into our new home right before Christmas, but I was lacking in Christmas spirit. I managed to get a Christmas tree up and decorated, and we celebrated with my parents and sisters. Overall, the holidays were a bit of a blur. I knew I was headed towards divorce and my husband was moving more than halfway across the country. I also knew being a single working mom would bring a whole new set of challenges, especially with a career that required travel. I'd worked hard and put in the extra effort to build a successful career, but now I was faced with a new ultimatum: dealing with things on my own. I was overwhelmed with the thought of being there for my children. I wanted to be a hands-on mom and still maintain the career I had worked so hard for. I began doubting my decisions, feeling guilty for failing to give my kids the upbringing I had envisioned. The truth is, I could feel myself teetering toward depression and a slump of self-disappointment. It was a very difficult point in my life. But it was also a turning point.

As a child, I dreamt of a happy and successful life. I wanted the perfect marriage, two kids, a house with the white picket fence, a great career, and the chance to travel and see the world. I was an ambitious dreamer. And while life didn't exactly go the way I'd dreamed or planned, I did achieve much of what I'd set my sights on. I am very fortunate and blessed to have two wonderful and loving children, an amazing family, and a rewarding career. I've had the chance to travel to many incredible places. I've had my share of successes and failures in life, but I always try to live life to the fullest. I credit my successes and accomplishments to three main things: 1) Confidence, which my parents instilled in me at a young age. I've always believed I could accomplish anything I set my mind to; 2) Goal setting—if you want to achieve your dreams, you need to set goals, then plan and pursue them relentlessly; and 3) Work ethic. You must be willing to put in the effort, hard work, and dedication to make things happen.

I specifically remember my mother telling me, "If you want to be the president of the United States, you can be." She made me realize I was in charge of my life. No one could hold me back.

My sisters and I were consistently reminded of our potential. We were told to work hard for what we wanted to achieve in life. I recognize not everyone is lucky enough to be raised with that support and encouragement. We all have different upbrings and family dynamics, and there is no perfect formula for creating confidence. My parents instilled love, confidence, and the importance of work ethic in all of us. I now see it was my upbringing that always propelled me to push forward and keep reaching for the stars, especially as a woman. If I could go back and talk to my younger self, I would tell her to dream bigger and go for it. I now believe that I could have, and should have, dreamed bigger. Sure, my childhood dreams might have seemed big enough—but now, I know there is no such thing as "A dream too big."

What Is Dreaming Big?

What does it mean to dream big? Ask five people and each will likely offer a different definition. For me, dreaming big means capturing the desire to believe you can create, experience, or achieve something new. This dream involves something that will truly make you happy and fulfilled. Dreaming big creates an inner drive to push yourself, discover yourself, and grow as you reach a specific goal or objective. Your dream keeps you focused and determined on your path to accomplishing personal and professional goals.

Consider these questions as you decide how big you want to dream:

- How can you discover your abilities and grow as a person unless you're willing to step in a new direction?
- How can you make yourself stand out in a crowd when you place limitations on yourself?
- How much regret will you have if you know you could have pursued bigger dreams, but chose not to?

When you are not bound by limitations, you will dream bigger. You'll know that you can do better than you are doing now, and that there is much more for you to accomplish.

Setting Goals to Achieve Your Dreams

Best-selling author Tony Robbins puts it this way: "Setting goals is the first step in turning the invisible into the visible." As I mentioned before, I've always loved setting goals. Anyone who has ever worked for me would tell you that. Goals are excellent for mapping out specific objectives you wish to achieve. These could include saving money, losing weight, going back to college to complete your degree, running a marathon, getting a new job or promotion, or buying a car or house. One of the most important aspects of goal setting is tuning into your intuitive compass of wants and desires. This way, you'll set goals that are important to *you*. You set the course, and you own the path to achieve your goal.

Years ago, I started a practice of working with my employees to set personal and professional goals. This was something I had done for myself every year, and it had helped me greatly. I instructed my employees to go through a simple exercise of five goal-setting steps:

1. Spend quality time thinking about what you want to accomplish this year.
2. Take time to write down your goals and aspirations.
3. Be specific about steps/actions you will take to achieve them.
4. Keep the list in a safe but visible place (I always suggest a copy in your wallet).
5. Revisit your goals on a regular basis to track progress and stay on course.

I would never ask my employees to share their personal goals because I believe those should remain private, but I did ask them to share their professional goals. By sharing them with me, I could understand what they wanted to achieve and support them in doing so.

One day, I was visiting one of my teams in Tampa, Florida, and I could see that a young man who had worked for me for two years was anxious to speak with me.

"Joanie, I have to tell you something," he said with joy in his voice. "Last year, you helped me with goal setting. I was living in an apartment, barely making ends meet." Obviously, I knew he had been successful at work over the last year and was consistently a strong performer. He went on to tell me that he was making more money than he had ever made, he'd saved enough to buy his first home, and he was about to buy a ring and propose to his girlfriend. He then opened his wallet and pulled out a piece of paper with his handwritten goals. The paper was worn around the edges, and you could tell it had been referred to many times. "Look at my goals," he said excitedly. I can't remember exactly what those black-inked words said, but it was something like this:

1. *Pay off credit card debt*
2. *Earn 100K*
3. *Buy my first house*
4. *Get engaged*

He proudly declared that he was on track to achieve each goal. He thanked me, and he was so heartfelt in telling me that his goals wouldn't have materialized unless he had taken the time to plan and write out what he wanted to accomplish, and then keep his goals in his wallet so he could continue working towards them. He was a true testament to the power of the approach. I was absolutely thrilled that he embraced the process and was achieving his goals.

The Foundational Fs

As years went by, I refined my goal-setting process for work and personal objectives. I would set goals around work promotions, sales achievements, buying a new home or car, exercise, savings, travel, vacations, family time, etc. I was always ambitious when it came to growing my career. At the same time, it was extremely important for me to focus on my family. I followed a simple approach towards setting and achieving personal goals which I refer to as the *Foundational Fs*: Faith, Family & Friends, Finance, Fitness, and FUN. Each F represents an important part of your life, and setting goals related to the Foundational Fs can help you achieve your best life.

Faith: Whether you are religious or spiritual is a personal preference. I think of faith as having dimensions beyond religion or spirituality. Faith is related to positive change that you and others can bring to your own life. If you are religious, faith could involve regular worship; if you are spiritual, you might have a regular meditation practice or like to spend time in nature. The faith component of achieving dreams can involve anything positive that helps you be your best self and achieve your big dreams. Faith provides a basis for setting personal goals that will facilitate your personal growth.

Family & Friends: The goals you specify in this aspect of your life can strengthen or build your relationships. Whether you establish these goals to benefit your relationship with your significant other, spouse, children, siblings, parents, friends, or other relationships, they all require your time and attention. Your goals regarding family could involve helping them cope with a difficult time, communicating with them more, or facilitating changes to solve problems. This aspect includes all you want to achieve for your family and friends.

Finance: Keeping your finances in order is a vital factor of success. That doesn't mean you must be wealthy—but you need enough to cover your expenses, save for the future, and enjoy vacations and other forms of entertainment. Your financial objectives should include all your personal and business objectives, such as investing in businesses or properties, buying your first home or retirement home, saving, and creating a career that will maximize your earnings. It's impossible to concentrate on something else in life when you are constantly worrying about finances and debts. Creating a financially stable life brings stability and alleviates stress.

Fitness: Improving your health and fitness will help you achieve your goals in other aspects of life. Without good health and fitness, you can't give 100 percent. Wealth and success mean nothing without good health. Doing everything possible to attain and enjoy your peak fitness level makes things more exciting. There are very few people with perfect health records, and for most, certain health problems cannot be entirely resolved regardless of how hard we work. But it certainly doesn't mean that we can't try to be at our best. We must set fitness goals that can help us work towards our best selves. Self-care is vital to our goals and the fulfillment of our lives.

Fun: Unfortunately, it's too easy to neglect fun while building a career. This aspect of life is just as important as all the others. Fun includes all the things that make you happy, bring you joy, and fulfill your purpose. Fun is the final aspect that ties together all the other Fs, and I would call it the most essential of the Fs. It's much easier to achieve if the first four Fs are already in order. There's no doubt in my mind that you—and I—were made to find, make, and enjoy as much fun and joy as possible.

Taking Care of Yourself

On that pivotal New Year's Eve, I thought of all the people I've helped with goal setting, and I suddenly realized I needed to take more of my own advice.

I decided to spend quality time writing down a statement detailing what I wanted to achieve and improve in each area. I needed to take time to reevaluate where I was in life and what I wanted to focus on. I wrote out specific "F" goals. I wrote: Family—ensure I have the proper care and attention for my children while I'm working. Find a wonderful nanny to help take care of them; Faith—we would attend Church on Sundays together; Finance —I would save a certain amount each month for my children's education; Fitness—we will eat balanced, healthy meals, and I will keep exercising four times a week; Fun—I would plan a vacation to take the kids to Disney World, just the three of us. It may sound simple, but I had to get the basics in place and focus on my priorities.

After I'd set my goals, I typed them up and printed three copies. I kept one in my wallet so I could always have them with me. I put the second copy on the inside of my closet door, so I could see them while I was getting dressed in the morning. I put the third copy in my journal, which I kept in my nightstand, so I could pray about them each night or morning and set my intentions for working towards my goals that day. I always kept those goals with me, and I am proud to say I achieved them.

I'd always heard that when you set goals you need to make them specific, measurable, attainable, and you must write them down and keep them visible. You might still get off track at times even if you do all that, but you can always adjust your goals as necessary. And there's no law that says you must check every box and achieve each goal perfectly every year. It might take years to achieve a goal. The idea is to keep your goals visible and keep working towards self-improvement. Doing so will help you stay focused on what is truly important to you.

I'd always wanted to run the New York City marathon, which was one of my "fitness" goals for many years. Sometimes, I laughed at myself for writing it down, but deep inside it was something I knew I wanted to achieve. Some years, there were reasons why I couldn't commit to it. Being a single mom with two young children and working full time doesn't give you a lot of free time to train for a marathon. Still, I kept it on the list, and eventually when my kids were older, I decided to go for it.

Running the NYC marathon was one of the best days of my life. I was fortunate to have family and friends come out to support me, and I enjoyed every step along the way. I loved seeing all the spectators lining the streets and cheering us runners on. It was a day I'll never forget, and I am so grateful that I made that commitment. I learned that if you want something badly enough and are willing to put in the effort, you can accomplish anything. I also learned to truly enjoy the experience. I don't just mean the final race—I had to enjoy the journey that came before achieving the goal. I enjoyed planning my runs, running for longer on weekends, and logging and tracking my progress. The entire experience was wonderful.

If you're like me, it can be easy to take life too seriously. Setting goals and achieving them can become grim and mechanical. Accomplishing objectives is much easier for me when I love what I'm doing. Many objectives aren't achieved because they aren't perceived as enjoyable—they're more like obligations. I credit a big part of my career success to the fact that I absolutely love what I do. It's easier to put in the effort and planning when you're dedicated and enjoy what you do.

When it comes to achieving goals, endurance is required. It's not just about building up physical endurance, it's about creating the mental toughness to overcome adversity and keep going. Webster's dictionary defines "endurance" as follows:

1. the ability to withstand hardship or adversity, *especially*: the ability to sustain a prolonged stressful effort or activity (ex: a marathon runner's *endurance*)
2. the act or an instance of enduring or suffering (ex: *endurance* of many hardships)
3. PERMANENCE, DURATION (ex: the *endurance* of the play's importance)

I find the definition of endurance sums up what it takes to achieve your personal and professional goals. Life is full of obstacles and hurdles that we must overcome. We all face adversity and challenges daily, and we need to find ways to manage. Life is not perfect—mine certainly is far from it. I needed to overcome adversity and find a way to create the life I wanted. That took endurance, mental toughness, grit, and confidence. Obstacles will never stop me from striving to do better, personally improving, living my best life, and doing the best job I can as a mom, daughter, friend, spouse, employee, boss, and Christian.

Is It Possible to Have It All?

Setting goals has helped me achieve many personal and professional successes. It has helped me organize my priorities and focus on important initiatives that I needed and wanted to do. I admit there are times I hold everything together with duct tape and rubber bands—but I still get it done. I also make time for myself to exercise, read, write, pray, and hang out with friends and family.

Trying to juggle a family and a career is a challenge for anyone. It's important to spend time identifying your top priorities and goals for your family *and* your career. Be realistic and specific about what is required and what you want to accomplish. Be clear about what you can and cannot do. Avoid taking on too much—otherwise you may set yourself up for failure. You might realize you need help or that you should start saying NO to certain things. Be reasonable and certain about what you can and cannot handle.

A few years ago, I began a new goal-setting practice that might be even more impactful. I reflected and wrote down all I was proud of accomplishing each year. The first year I did it, I ended up with a few pages of reflections. It forced me to take a moment and appreciate myself. As a busy working mom, it's rare to pat yourself on the back and appreciate all you do for everyone else. Recognizing all the positive contributions I made over the past year was a meaningful exercise. I encourage everyone to do it. *Especially* women.

Over ten years have passed since that difficult New Year's Eve. I will never forget that turning point in my life. I am grateful for the incredible support and guidance I have received from my family, friends, and mentors. I am especially thankful for the practice of reflecting on my accomplishments and setting aspirations, intentions, and goals for the new year.

I hope my story encourages you to focus on dreaming big, prioritizing what's important, and achieving personal and professional success. Search your soul for inspiration. Dig deep and push to understand what is most important to you. Most of all, believe in yourself. You can accomplish amazing things. Don't give up on your dreams for yourself, your family, or your career. As they say, life is a marathon, not a sprint. Make sure you build your endurance to keep yourself on track. And remember, it's never too late to DREAM BIG!

CHAPTER FOUR REFLECTION

If you want to live your best career and life, it's important to dream beyond where you are now. You need to set goals that will get you moving towards a bigger, better future. Goals and planning are essential to being successful in any endeavor and in life. Start by making a list of your priorities. What's most important to you right now? Reflect on these questions to begin planning and taking steps towards achieving your goals, keep it in a visible place, and tell people about your plan.

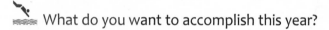 What do you want to accomplish this year?

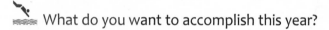 What are your goals and aspirations?

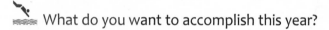 What specific steps or actions will you take to achieve them?

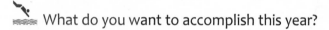 How often will you revisit your plan and how will you track your progress?

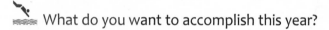 What are your foundational "F" (Faith, Family, Friends, Finance, Fitness, & Fun) goals this year? Write them down and keep them with you.

STRATEGY 2

EXPERIENCE:
USE THE SPRINGBOARD

CARPE DIEM! MAKE THE MOST OF EARLY WORK EXPERIENCE

"Information is not knowledge. The only source of knowledge is experience. You need experience to gain wisdom."
– Albert Einstein

Prior to the pandemic, you might have experienced a group of fresh young interns getting an introductory company tour, clutching their notepads or laptops, and taking notes on the go. Usually around mid-May, a class of interns would appear excited, bright, and frightened all at the same time. Though many interns have since been working remotely, I do predict the in-person intern programs to return.

Internships are invaluable. Not only do they provide students with real life work experience, but it's also a great way for students to test the waters on a short-term basis while also building their resumes. In Chapter 1, "Test the Waters & Find Purpose," I wrote about my son, Chase, who is studying Golf Management in college. He just completed his first golf internship, and I am so proud of how hard he worked. He made sure he showed up on time every day, and he was always prepared to make the most of the opportunity. He will be required to complete four different internships before he graduates, so he will be building his work experience and testing the waters in different opportunities in golf.

On his second day of the internship at the golf course, he told me, "Mom, so far, I love it. I feel at home here."

He not only enjoyed the experience, but he was able to visualize himself in a rewarding career in the field. The internship was further validation that he is on the right career path.

Writing about internships takes me back to my own first internship, which was with the U.S. Customs Service at JFK Airport in New York. As a student majoring in Health and Human Services at the State University of New York, the opportunity to train and assimilate disabled individuals allowed me to test my passion for training and working with new employees. As part of that experience, I attended their new-hire training and helped new employees onboard into their new roles. Not only did I take to that role, but I also found it fascinating to observe how the U.S. Customs Service conducted training. Stories from customs agents left me wide-eyed, as did getting used to the novelty of a workplace that included drug-sniffing German Shepherds. It's hard to understate how excited I was to have my first opportunity to be in a professional work environment.

Like most interns, I wanted to do the best job I could and make a lasting impression. After all, you never know where an internship might lead. My good friend Gwen and I had the opportunity to tackle this assignment together. We learned about the role of US Customs and what they did to keep drugs from coming into our country at one of the busiest airports in the world. We took our roles very seriously, and we also welcomed the opportunity to learn more than just the work that was required of us. We learned about the agency, how things worked, and what the agents were trained to look for. We asked lots of questions. It was a fascinating experience, and I am so grateful I took the chance to immerse myself in the work and make the most of the internship.

One of my favorite sayings has always been *Carpe Diem*. I'm sure you know it means "seize the day." I think it's a very appropriate saying and meaning for an internship—or really for any work experience. Seize the opportunity to make your future better.

During my career, I've also had the pleasure of working for several companies that have embraced and welcomed college students to intern with us over their summer breaks. I always smile when I see a new class of interns all bright eyed, buttoned up, and nervous on their orientation day. Of the hundreds of interns I've interacted with over the years, several have stood out and created a lasting positive impression. Maybe it's the questions they ask, the way they carry themselves, or their personal communication skills. In this chapter, you'll learn how to be one of those interns who is recognized and remembered.

If you are a college student or in a professional grad school like law school or business school, you should fill your summers with meaningful work experiences. While scoring an internship may—or may not—be difficult (depending on where you live and the state of the economy), it's crucial to at least find a summer internship that will advance or clarify your career goals. Achieving that objective requires strategy, effort, and energy. You'll also need a sense of urgency, passion, and great networking skills.

My focus here is to offer some practical advice for those who are in college or early in their career. Once again, let's dive in D.E.E.P.!

How to Find Internships and Early Work Experience:

Tip 1. Get Strategic: Before you start looking for work, consider what you want to get out of the experience by asking yourself the following questions:

- What skills do I want to acquire and/or develop?
- How are the skills I already have applicable to marketing myself to companies and recruiters?
- What don't I want to do during an internship experience?
- What are my "dream" companies that I'd absolutely love to work for?
- Do I need or want academic credit for my internship?
- Can I afford to volunteer for an internship, or do I need to earn a salary?
- Do I want to intern remotely or in person? If in person, where?
- What types of positions do I want to explore during an internship?
- Would I like to work in a larger organization with a team of other interns? Or would I rather be the only intern or one among a few interns?
- Do I want to position myself for a future job with the company I'm interning at? Or am I only exploring job functions, employers, and skills at this point?

Tip 2. Stay Ahead of the Curve: Internships tend to have a specific time-sensitive trajectory. Larger companies may begin the recruiting, interviewing, and hiring processes as early as August of the year before, while smaller companies may not get going until the winter or early spring. The earlier you are ready to begin your search for an internship, the better. Be prepared with an updated resume, LinkedIn profile, and elevator pitch (personal introduction) by the end of summer the year *before* you want to intern. Answer the questions outlined in Tip 1 and know what you want to accomplish.

Tip 3. Connect with Your Support System: If you haven't yet established a relationship with your career services office, get in there, introduce yourself, and find out how they support students in seeking internships. Make an appointment with your academic advisor and/or favorite professors to discuss your options. Listen to any suggestions they may have. Talk to your parents about connecting with their friends and colleagues. See how you might leverage their networks to find internship opportunities. Reach out to recruiters and sign up with temporary staffing agencies. They are a great source of local temporary jobs.

Tip 4. Get Organized: Create an organizational system—such as a Google Sheets or Excel spreadsheet—to stay on top of your search. This system should include the names of companies with internship opportunities, the names and contact information of recruiters and hiring managers, internship deadlines, and other critical information related to your internship search.

How to Identify Opportunities

A successful candidate employs every tool at their disposal to build relationships for the present and future and find opportunities that will illuminate their career path. The skills and motivation that will help you land a great internship will also serve you in your first job out of school.

These next few tips will help you translate the skills and experience you've gained in school into a rewarding, meaningful career.

Tip 1. Stake Out Your Digital Presence: Believe it or not, chaos lurks directly behind the seemingly impenetrable doors of the companies you're trying to get into. Larger companies are posting jobs on different job boards, but they also have their own career sites that you ought to scour. You need to cast a wide digital net to be found online. Leverage LinkedIn by optimizing your profile, connections, and the site's job search feature. If you don't have a LinkedIn profile, create one now. You'll want to build a professional online profile of your education and work experience so employers can find you. (I will talk more about building your professional brand in Chapter 10, "Brand YOU.") There are dozens of other career sites out there—try some of those too. Companies and career sites will want your resume, so if you haven't updated it, now's the time. Apply online with local temporary staffing agencies and reach out to local recruiters.

Tip 2. Get Connected: Start with your educational institution. Talk to your professors and career advisors about available opportunities. Recruiters often hold career fairs at schools, so there's an established relationship there. Personal recommendations count for a lot with most companies, so figure out if your school, advisor, professor, or other mentors will come through for you. Alumni of your school can also help. They're often motivated to help a job seeker who attended their alma mater, and they are easy to identify through LinkedIn or your school's career/alumni office. Ask your parents to introduce you to their professional contacts and help you search for opportunities. Put the word out to everyone you know—including on Facebook, Instagram, or other social networks. Networking is vital, and referrals are one of the best ways to land a job. Remember: looking for a job is a full-time job.

Tip 3. Demonstrate Persistence: No two recruiters and hiring managers are alike. Some are well-organized, while others are not. Don't limit yourself to one method of communication or outreach. Once you're aware of opportunities, connect with companies, recruiters, and hiring managers through as many channels as possible. Once you get a response, use that channel (unless they steer you toward another). Sending a single note and expecting to get results doesn't work in today's fast-paced world. Make sure you are consistent in your search and follow-up on every possible lead.

Tip 4. Prepare Like a Pro: Develop an elevator pitch outlining your character traits, skills, and the value you will provide to a company. Research the company and prepare a list of questions that you can ask towards the end of the interview. An internship can be the stepping-stone to a future full-time position with the company, so treat it like a real job interview.

Examples of interview prep questions that you can ask include:

- Can you share or describe the responsibilities of the position?
- How would you describe a typical day and week in this position?
- What experience or skills are you looking for in an intern?
- What would you say are the biggest challenges of this job?
- Is overtime expected?
- Can you describe the company culture?

Tip 5: Stay Positive: A positive and upbeat attitude is crucial when networking and interviewing for a summer internship—or any job opportunity, for that matter. Companies are attracted to positive people who bring a fresh and new perspective to the work environment. So, get out there and sell yourself. Good luck, and have fun with it!

How to Optimize Your Internship or First Job

By now, let's assume you've landed your internship or first job. The next step is to make sure you make the most of it. This is your chance to learn what you like or don't like about the organization and industry. Strive to get the most out of the experience. And stay positive.

Here are a few Dos and Don'ts to help you make the most of your internship or early work experience. (If you're an employer with interns working for you, these tips may help you coach them.)

Dos

Prework: What separates the interns who listlessly pass through an office from the ones who make a name for themselves? For starters: Preparation. Smart interns spend time reading up on the company they're about to work for. They monitor the social channels. They read about the company's executives to find things they have in common, like schools, hobbies, or organizations. If you notice commonalities, just be careful with your approach so you don't look like you're "sucking up" or stalking. It may be summer, but you still must do your homework!

Network: It's time to start building your professional network and connections on LinkedIn. It's not simply a matter of learning a name and sending an invite. You need to form a human connection first. Treat everyone with courtesy and respect. The positive interactions you make today could be references or recommendations that will benefit you tomorrow. The best part is that connections work both ways, meaning they'll see you as an investment in their future. Maybe one day they'll say, "I knew you when ..."

Raise Your Hand: Yes, do the job you've been tasked with. But also take the initiative to go the extra mile. Folding, filing, stapling, and copying may be required. After that, do *more*. Raise your hand. Volunteering to stay late to work on a project that wasn't assigned to you demonstrates resourcefulness. There's a caveat here: be wary of expressing your enthusiasm out in the open too much.

Keep Track: Keep a journal. It doesn't matter whether it's on your laptop or in a notebook. The point is that you document what you do every day. Don't expect to remember what you just learned three months from now— you won't, and you certainly won't have captured all the minute details. Periodically add the results of your efforts to your journal and online profile. Ask your supervisor or higher-ups for a recommendation, comment, or testimonial regarding your contribution. This will be great for your LinkedIn page and your resume.

Be Ready: Your first day will be all about meet and greets. But Human Resources (HR) will require you to fill out forms so you can satisfy regulatory requirements, get paid, have taxes withheld, etc. Find out what's required before you show up on the first day. Even in our digitized world, you'll need physical identification documents such as your Social Security card, birth certificate, driver's license, or passport to start your internship.

Expect The Unexpected: Be prepared. Bring a laptop with you just in case your assigned device isn't ready. It happens. Also, bring a pen and notepad with you. Information that might be critical to your assignment's success may be provided, and you'll want to jot it down. Prepare your attire the night before to ensure you're ready to go. Dress like the people you've met during the interview process. In the morning, leave for work twice as early as you think you need to. Showing up late and sweating is no way to start.

Give it Your Best: Give every assignment your absolute best. What you do with little things shows management how you will perform more important/larger tasks. Take initiative to go above and beyond what is asked of you.

Communicate & Send Thank You Notes: Who writes handwritten notes anymore? Who takes the time to write something poetic and meaningful on stationary, addressed by hand, with the postage to imply that you walked to a mailbox? You can certainly share your thanks electronically, but be sure to also follow up with a detailed letter that someone can physically hold. Keep it simple. Single out something you learned from them that you'll take with you. Not just an assignment, but something that made this person's influence memorable. Never underestimate the value of a handwritten thank you note.

Be Present: Most importantly, be alert and engaged. Get your head out of your smartphone. Be present in all conversations. Show interest and ask questions, but don't try to answer any before you understand. Let your actions do the talking. You also want your supervisor to feel like they were successful in identifying you as a good prospect, so be appreciative of any duties assigned to you along the way.

Don'ts

Be Late or Invisible: Show up a few minutes early every day. Don't disappear during the day. Check in first thing in the morning, at lunch, and before you leave in the evening. If you're going to be late, use two methods of communication. Give advanced notice if you have a doctor's appointment. Adopting this practice early will benefit your career in the long run.

Talk Behind Backs: Religion and politics are well-established no-nos. The same is true for gossiping about your coworkers. There's an old rule about people who talk behind other people's backs: they're probably doing the same thing to you. Your supervisor may do it. Your closest work friends may do it. That doesn't mean you should. Plus, you can guarantee it will almost always get back to someone. Do yourself a favor—don't go there.

Post About Your Job: Most workplaces have a sanctioned social media account. Be careful when it comes to posting or sharing information about your employer and your job. Check the employee guide, which applies to you, to understand what the company considers acceptable information to share. Clients consider the work you do for them confidential, and so should you. Even if someone else is doing it, don't risk ending up in hot water.

The kiss of death is to ask/say:

- "When will I get more important things to do?"
- "What do I have to do to get an important project?"
- "I'll take work seriously when it's a real/permanent job."

Many interns have left a lasting impression on me over the years, specifically those who clearly took the opportunity very seriously and made a point to connect with me. Some of them truly possessed impeccable follow-up skills. A few have even stayed in touch with me to this day.

A young man named Brian particularly comes to mind. I met Brian on his first day at Monster Worldwide. He made a point of introducing himself to me. During his time at Monster, he would ask me questions and for advice. He was always professional and so curious about business and marketing. Towards the end of his internship, he asked if he could connect with me on LinkedIn and stay in touch.

Not only did Brian connect with me, but he sent me a handwritten thank you note for spending time with him and taking him under my wing. He also continued to stay in touch with me, sometimes commenting on different posts I made or dropping me a note. It's no surprise that Brian did this with many colleagues at Monster and ended up landing a great job at their offices after college. He tried his hardest to network, learn, and make the most of his internship experience, and it paid off for him. It has been fun to watch him advance his career and continue to achieve success.

Over the years, I have admired interns and their eagerness to learn and experience as much as they could. I have valued their insights and perspective on what they observed. They bring fresh perspective, and there is always an opportunity to learn from them as well.

CHAPTER FIVE REFLECTION

Getting early work experience is an essential aspect of starting a successful career, especially in a field that aligns with your interests, skills, and values. The earlier you start gaining experience, the better. Not only does it help demonstrate your commitment and capabilities to an employer, but it is a great way to "test the waters" and find your ideal career path. When exploring potential internship or volunteer opportunities, start by answering these questions for yourself:

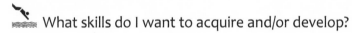 What skills do I want to acquire and/or develop?

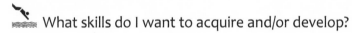 What are my "dream" companies that I'd love to work for?

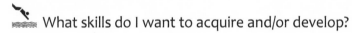 Do I need/want academic credit for my internship? Do I need a salary, or can I afford to volunteer?

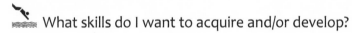 What types of positions do I want to explore during an internship or volunteer position?

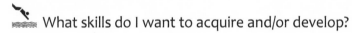 Who can I network with to find leads and opportunities?

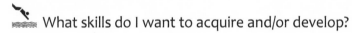 Create professional online profiles and apply with staffing agencies.

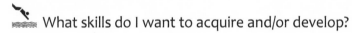 Consider temporary/contract work to get your foot in the door. It is a great way to gain experience and start building connections.

EMBRACE MENTORSHIP

"I am a firm believer that you don't achieve greatness on your own. There is always someone there to lend a hand."
– Greg Louganis, Five-Time Gold Medal Olympic Diver

When Rose—a bright, talented, up-and-coming marketing professional who worked for one of the top IT staffing companies in the country—asked me to become her mentor, I accepted immediately. Though I was extremely busy with my own career, I was honored that she had asked me to take on this special role for her career development. The situation was somewhat unusual. Rose was participating in a mentorship program at her organization that typically involved in-house mentors. Because Rose and I had a close relationship from our time with a prior employer, she asked for, and received, special permission to work with me as an outside mentor.

During a lunch to initiate the in-person component of the mentor relationship, Rose explained the details of her mentor program to me. The program involved meeting once a month in person, plus two phone calls a month. Rose then began to update me on her current role, explaining what she was working on and the challenges she was facing.

"Joanie, when I attend meetings with my boss and team, I don't feel like I'm on an equal playing field," she said with an uneasy expression on her face.

"What exactly do you mean by that?" I probed.

"When I'm in meetings with the CEO and vice presidents, I always listen closely to their requests and ideas and then follow up with solutions to those problems."

"Rose, when you step into a meeting, do you come prepared with your own advice and recommendations?"

"No," she admitted. "To be honest, I spend more of my time answering their requests and following up on their ideas and questions."

"Let's try this," I said. "During the next meeting, I want you to walk into the room with your expert hat on. You need to tell yourself, 'I am the marketing expert, and I am here to offer my advice and counsel on this topic.' You know marketing and public relations better than anyone else in that room."

"Okay," she said. It was clear she was thinking deeply about what I'd said.

"Remember, marketing is your area of expertise!" I emphasized. "When you attend the meeting, make sure you have an opportunity to share some recommendations and ideas. Be prepared to go to the meeting with a few things to suggest and the reasons why you're suggesting them."

"What else should I do?" Rose asked, fully engaged with my idea.

"Bring data to back up your recommendations," I replied. "You've been put in this position to be the authority. They will listen to you. Just make sure you're prepared and confident. Do you think you can do that?"

"Yes," she answered. She was nodding confidently now. "Great idea! Can we schedule a follow-up call so I can let you know how it goes?"

"Absolutely!" I said, taking out my calendar app so we could schedule a date and time.

At the appointed time and date a few weeks later, I picked up the phone to hear from an upbeat and newly confident Rose.

"Joanie, I took your advice. In my last meeting with my CEO, I let him know that I had some recommendations I wanted to share with him and the team," she reported excitedly.

"The team listened to my ideas and gave me some great feedback. They also thanked me for my advice and said that they would like to move forward with some of my ideas. I think this could be a real game-changer for me. I felt more equal to the others in the room. And I felt a big boost of confidence when they gave me productive feedback and talked through the details of executing on a couple of my ideas."

"Good job," I said with a smile.

After hanging up, I leaned back in my chair and thought about the Rose I knew and appreciated from our time working together. A diligent worker who never let anything fall through the cracks, Rose was organized, detail-oriented, and what I would consider a perfectionist. She also was creative, innovative, and worked well with others. Like many women, Rose had a strong desire to please her superiors. She wanted to excel in her job. My concern was that she wasn't establishing a platform to share her innovative ideas and creativity. I also realized she needed a little confidence boost to feel comfortable at the table with her boss and coworkers. My pushing her a bit on this issue led to immediate success. I was so happy for her.

I could tell how gratified she was by the positive reception to her advice. We talked about her continuing to take time to prepare for the meetings. I emphasized that she should remain confident and strong in her voice and her recommendations, focusing on the value she could bring to her work and the company.

As the mentorship progressed, Rose came to realize that her job was to be the authority in her area of expertise, sharing the best advice that she possibly could. With her growing confidence, her engagement in work accelerated. Of course, that didn't mean more challenges wouldn't appear.

A few months later, Rose and I went for lunch. I immediately noticed she looked troubled.

"What's going on, Rose?" I asked. "Is everything okay?"

"I've realized that all the other managers who report directly to the CEO have vice president titles," she said. "But I still have a manager title. That doesn't seem right, especially since I'm the only woman. I believe I've proven my value, and my advice has helped increase company sales. You know how important it is for me to advance my career, increase my income, and get promoted. I don't want my career to stagnate or to feel like I'm less valuable to the company just because I'm a woman."

"Rose," I replied. "Your words are music to my ears. There's no doubt in my mind that you deserve a raise and a promotion. Let's brainstorm and do what we can to get your boss on board! To start, let's list what you've accomplished in your current role and consider how you've added value since you've been there."

We made a list of her various contributions and current responsibilities. As homework, I advised her to consider how she'd like to expand her role to benefit the organization. Since she was seeking a raise and a promotion, she needed to come up with a few strong ideas for how her role could expand. I further recommended that she request a meeting with her boss to discuss her progress, role, and the next steps to advance her career.

The day of Rose's meeting with her boss, I was on pins and needles. No, it wasn't my meeting—but Rose was a great friend and a special person. I so wanted her to receive the promotion and raise she deserved.

When the phone rang, I grabbed it and said, "Rose! How did the meeting go?"

"I got a raise and a promotion to director!" she said.

"How phenomenal!" I was so excited.

"And there's more. To build out on some of my ideas, I was given the go-ahead to add a marketing manager to my team!"

Looking back now at the experience of coaching and mentoring Rose, I know what she needed most was confidence. She needed the confidence to be herself and sell her ideas. She needed the confidence to share her well-thought-out ideas. She needed the confidence to flex her knowledge in meetings when it came to areas where she was the expert. She needed the confidence to have uncomfortable conversations and to ask for what she wanted. Building confidence is critical in the relationship between mentor and mentee.

Why Mentors and Mentoring Are Important

Mentors (and the mentoring process) build better employees, leaders, and organizations. In fact, 67 percent of organizations report increases in productivity related to mentoring, while 55 percent of companies believe that mentoring is positively correlated with increased profitability.[21] The experience of being mentored is a very positive one: mentees are promoted five times more often than those without mentors, while 25 percent of employees enrolled in a mentoring program receive salary grade increases (compared to just 5 percent who aren't mentored).[22] Finally, mentoring programs are directly and positively related to talent retention. Millennials who plan on remaining employed at their current organization for more than five years are twice as likely to have a mentor.[23] Reasons millennials quit their job include the lack of advancement, learning, and development opportunities.[24]

Mentoring and being mentored have had a major impact on my life and my career. I've been lucky to have had some exceptional mentors in my life. Mentors provide a wonderful sounding board to discuss challenges and roadblocks and to share experiences. We can all learn from others who are in a different place in their career arc. They can share wisdom on what they've learned and answer the following questions:

- What worked?
- What didn't?
- What would they do differently?
- What would they recommend?

In some cases, a formal mentoring relationship (such as coaching) can help guide you to grow and develop to a higher level. In other cases, an informal or unofficial mentor may work better. You may have a peer or colleague who can provide advice and coaching. Maybe you have people you admire who you can reach out to with questions or ask for advice as needed. You don't need to have an official program in place for someone to mentor and coach you. Either way, I advise you to embrace it! Embrace people you admire and want to learn from. Ask them questions about their experiences and their journey. Learn from their successes and mistakes.

How to Leverage a Mentor

Many years ago, I was asked to take on a new role at my company. This job involved a two-year special project focusing on innovating and realigning how the company went to market. To take on this role, I would have to relinquish my current job running a large P&L over $300 million in revenue. I really enjoyed this role, and I wasn't sure I wanted to step away from my team. Adding to my hesitation was the fact that this new position would be a completely different role. As it was described to me, I would be leading a team tasked with designing a transformational business model for the entire organization. Should I take on this role, my new team would be working with a group of consultants to document the current state of the business, what challenges the organization faced, and what opportunities lay on the horizon. We would be tasked with designing a completely new model from soup to nuts, including the technology platforms that would power this new operating model. Once the new model was up and running, we would then pilot the program in a few markets before rolling it out across the country.

While I was intrigued by the idea of having so much say in the future direction of the company, I also was wary of sacrificing my position as a leader with a thriving operating division. All too often, women are sidelined into non-operating businesses such as marketing or human resources. Since P&L management experience is a critical stepping-stone to the top ranks of the largest and most successful organizations, relinquishing this experience ultimately hurts our prospects for advancement to the C-Suite.

Before I made my decision, I decided to speak with a colleague I admired and trusted. Sherry was about 20 years my senior with a successful track record in business. A veteran of different business units across the company, Sherry was also a great sounding board who knew my strengths and weaknesses.

In a frank conversation about my current and potential future roles, she asked me several penetrating questions, including:

- What would be the benefits of the role?
- What new skills would I learn?
- What would this role prepare me for in the future?
- What would happen if I didn't take the role?

After we talked, I thought through her questions. Reflecting on them, I realized this would be a stretch assignment for me (I'll talk more about stretch assignments in Chapter 7). The role would give me the opportunity to collaborate with a prestigious group of consultants—top in their field. Through this collaboration, I would be exposed to some of the best critical thinkers in the industry. Coordinating their work and the work of my team would allow me to develop new project management skills that weren't required in my current position. Building new skills would improve my leadership capabilities and my strategic planning expertise. I also realized I would be sacrificing a huge opportunity if I turned down the role—I would be giving up the potential to have a major impact on the future design of the organization. Looking ahead, I could envision how executing this role well could set me up for a larger role with the organization down the road.

I called Sherry to update her on my thoughts. We agreed to meet for coffee.

"Joanie, I think this is definitely a stretch assignment for you," she said. "You'll probably never have another opportunity or role like this. But you will also never go back to the role you're currently in. If you take on this assignment, I can see it propelling you towards further growth here at this company or in another organization."

After a few more days spent pondering the pros and cons of this move, I decided to go ahead and take the opportunity. Consulting with Sherry was wise. I needed to see this opportunity from the perspective of someone with more experience to help me analyze my options. In hindsight, Sherry was right. My new role was a stretch assignment. It tested me and taught me a whole new set of skills that helped me prepare for future roles. Taking on that project transformed me into a more strategic thinker and collaborative leader. Today, I am so glad I made that choice. And I am thankful for the coaching and guidance Sherry shared with me.

The Value of a Mentoring Culture

Throughout my career, I've admired many female leaders with the ability to balance work and motherhood. Naturally, I hitched my wagon to their advice and any nuggets of wisdom they would share.

There came another time when Sherry shared some advice with me. One day, we were talking about balancing career and family and the struggles of traveling with little kids.

"Joanie, no matter what you do, make sure you always plan two great vacations a year with your kids," she said. Sherry had raised two boys alongside a demanding career, but she'd *always* managed to take two vacations a year and create lasting memories with her kids when they were younger. She encouraged me to create experiences and memories my children would always remember. She encouraged me to get my kids involved in the planning process and to also make sure they knew these vacations were benefits of mom working. Her advice stayed with me. It still does today.

Another wonderful mentor and former boss, Genia, shared advice with me about the importance of self-care. She said the best gift I could give my children was to be healthy and be there for them. "Get all your doctors' appointments and your mammogram completed by your birthday every year," she advised. "Don't ever skip doctor appointments. Your health and welfare are the best gift you can give your kids." That piece of advice has never strayed from my thoughts. I have received great guidance and advice from official mentors and unofficial mentors, and I couldn't be more thankful.

Years ago, I was at a crossroads after being recruited for executive positions in the employment industry. I had always wanted to be a CEO, but I also knew that as the mother of two school-age children, the demands of the C-Suite and its heavy travel schedule would pose challenges. As eager as I was to take the next step in my career, setting realistic boundaries and expectations would be critical to ensuring that my next role was a success.

One of the positions I was considering involved significant overseas travel. While I felt well-qualified for the position, I realized that extended, frequent overseas travel while parenting two young children would stretch my capacities too far. I made the choice to pass on the position to ensure that both my personal and professional life were sustainable in the short and long term.

While I was disappointed to walk away from that job, I was fortunate enough to gain another opportunity to run a staffing business in the United States. Although travel was required for this position, I believed it was something I could balance. There were at least, for me, reasonable geographical boundaries. As part of my consideration of that offer, I reached out to my good friend and mentor Joyce Russell to ask for advice. She has a long and successful track record of being the president of a large company, and she's raised two boys. Because of her experience juggling parenting and executive roles, I felt she would be a great sounding board for me.

"Joyce," I said, "I'm a bit nervous because this role would require a tremendous amount of responsibility and travel. Expectations are high, and I know the position will be demanding. I'm just not sure I can pull it off given the kids and everything I've got going on at home."

"Joanie, if this is the job you want, go for it," Joyce replied. "The important thing is to make sure you have the right support system around you so that you can maximize your effectiveness at work and at home."

"With the bump in compensation, you can afford to hire help to drive the kids to school or activities," she continued. "Consider getting a housekeeper or personal assistant to help you stay on top of everything."

As we talked, Joyce encouraged me to outsource as much as possible—housework, food shopping, errands, etc.

"Don't spend your downtime in the evenings and weekends on all the chores that didn't get done during the week," she cautioned, laughing. She knew me all too well!

While it was great to hear her perspective—advice I knew I needed—I still had to wrap my head around the idea of asking others for help. Maybe it's a challenge of wanting to do it all, of feeling like I shouldn't have to ask for others to help me get things done. I needed to give myself permission to ask for help. In fact, I had to understand that getting help was critical for me to succeed both in my next career and as a parent. No one can do everything.

By outsourcing many mundane activities such as housework and errands, I could then spend my free time and weekends with my family and friends, living a more balanced life. Taking Joyce's advice literally changed my life. I became comfortable asking for help, which enabled me to get the support I needed to succeed at home and at work.

I'm so grateful to Joyce for giving me permission to hire additional help. If I was going to take the next big job, I needed it. I valued and respected her sound advice immensely—and it made me realize that just because I wanted it all, didn't mean I had to do everything myself. The best mentors, like Joyce, inspire me to be the best version of myself.

Having mentors and being a mentor is rewarding in so many ways. I have had both male and female mentors and coaches, and I have learned from them all. I would not be where I am today without their wisdom, guidance, and advice.

Mentorship works. I'm certain of that. I encourage everyone to be a mentor to a colleague, student, or intern. You may never know the role you play in someone's life, but you can make a difference. Plus, it's rewarding and can help someone achieve greater success in life. We can accomplish so much more by supporting one another and sharing our wisdom.

Rose and I recently connected again at an industry event. I was not surprised to learn she'd been promoted to a vice president role and was also growing her team and responsibility. I thought to myself: Watching someone else advance their career and achieve their goals is more rewarding than advancing my own career. Hence my desire to write and publish this book!

CHAPTER SIX REFLECTION

Mentorship and coaching can be instrumental in gaining satisfaction, enjoyment, and success out of your career, and can lead to more promotions and salary increases. We can all learn from those who are in a different place in their career how to navigate challenges, and eventually we can provide valuable advice and guidance of our own. In some cases, a formal mentoring relationship (such as coaching) can help guide you to grow and develop to a higher level. In other cases, an informal or unofficial mentor may work better. Either way, I advise you to embrace the opportunity!

What mentors have you had in the past? What did you learn from them?

Who do you admire, and would they be willing to mentor or coach you?

Would they be willing and able to challenge you to improve, ask tough questions, and deliver real feedback (positive and negative)?

Based on your career ambitions, who can help you achieve those goals?

Where do you have an opportunity to mentor or coach others?

CHAPTER 7

STRETCH & TAKE THE LEAP

"If you're offered a seat on a rocket ship, don't ask, 'What seat?' Just get on."
– Sheryl Sandberg

Knee deep in my to-do list, I picked up my ringing office phone.

"Joanie, I need some help," said Anthony, the new company marketing director. "How would you feel about being on television and filling in for our CEO on a news segment tomorrow?"

He sounded anxious.

"Tig is scheduled to be on TV to discuss the latest job data, but something else came up on his schedule that he can't cancel, so now he's not available for the live interview," Anthony added. "The segment will be filmed at the network's studio in Manhattan. We've worked hard to build this relationship with the network. We can't cancel on them with less than 24-hour notice. If we do, I'm concerned we won't get invited back."

"I am so flattered that you even thought of me," I replied. "But I've never been on national TV. I'm not sure I would be the best person to fill in for Tig."

Though I may have sounded calm, my inner alarm bells were ringing. Tig, our CEO, was a phenomenal speaker. He appeared regularly on all the national news networks. Not only was he smart and sophisticated, but he was also clearly a subject matter expert. When he spoke, people paid attention. But with me? Not so much.

All I could think was: *Oh no. How could I ever fill in for him?*

"Joanie, you've got this," Anthony said confidently. "Don't you remember how you aced our PR training a few months ago? The entire PR team was so impressed by your performance in mock interviews. A 'natural' was what I believe they called you."

"That's very kind," I said. "But I still think it's a big reach for me to replace our CEO."

"No, no, not at all!" he exclaimed. "Our PR agency and team gave you a big vote of confidence. They think you'll be perfect. It's also a great opportunity for you to upgrade your skills and create more visibility for yourself and the company. We'll help you prepare. I'll even come with you to the studio."

"All right," I said, surrendering gracefully.

Accepting Challenges

When this opportunity arose, I could have declined the offer and stayed in my safe place. As Anthony worked on persuading me, thoughts were running through my head:

- Should I try something new?
- Should I be vulnerable and put myself out there to be interviewed on live TV?

- What if I freeze and forget what to say?
- What if I say the wrong thing and I get fired from my current job?
- What if I wake up with a big pimple on my nose?

You get the idea. It's easy to second-guess myself, take the easy way out, and avoid risk. It was a moment I was familiar with. Should I dive into the pool or let fear hold me back? While I knew I would be nervous, Anthony was so convincing that I decided to say yes. I decided to feel the fear and dive in.

Anthony was thrilled I'd agreed. He promised to send over some talking points to help me prepare. He also said he would call me that night so we could role play some questions and go over a few pointers.

I studied and prepared like I was going to take a college final exam. I knew my material inside and out. I picked out a special outfit to wear and made sure I went to bed at a decent hour to get a good night's sleep. Of course, my nerves interfered with my sleep, but I tried.

The next day, I traveled into midtown Manhattan and arrived at the studio with Anthony. We checked in at the front desk, and then a staffer came down to walk us through security and into the green room.

"I'm Carly," she said, shaking my hand. "It's great to have you here!"

I smiled as both Anthony and I greeted her.

As we walked over to the greenroom, Carly asked, "What are you going to be discussing today?"

"Employment trends and the latest job data," I replied.

"That's important—we need to know what those numbers mean. It sounds like you're the best expert to translate that for us," she said. "I'll let hair and makeup know that you're here."

She left us in the greenroom, and before I knew it, I was getting my makeup and hair touched up. Next, they showed me into the freezing cold studio, where I took a seat at the table with the anchor. They were on a commercial break, and I introduced myself. The anchor couldn't have been nicer. She said she was so glad I was able to fill in and that they were excited to have me on set. I just hoped I wasn't shaking from being cold or too nervous.

As she was talking, the sound technician quickly set up my earpiece and microphone. It all happened so fast. Next thing I knew, the producers were saying: "30 seconds to live ... 15 seconds ... 5 ... and we are LIVE!"

And then the intro music started.

I only had one second to think: *Oh no ... what have I just gotten myself into!* before the anchor introduced me and the conversation began to roll.

Luckily for me, my five minutes of fame flew by. I focused my attention on the conversation with the anchor, answering her questions to the best of my ability. I didn't think about the cameras or how many people might be watching. I knew I had a job to do, and I didn't want to let Anthony, my CEO, or my company down. When the interview ended, I could still feel my heart beating through my chest—but then the technicians quickly removed my mic and wires, and the anchor thanked me for coming on the show. It was over. A wave of relief washed over me. I walked back to the greenroom where Anthony was waiting for me.

"You knocked it out of the park," he said enthusiastically. "You were fantastic. I told you that you would be a natural at this."

Because it all happened so fast, it was hard for me to know how I'd really done on TV. Even now, I can't say I remember what I said or how I answered the questions. I thanked Anthony for his kind words and the opportunity to be the CEO's stand-in. I also thanked him for pushing me out of my comfort zone and making me put myself out there.

I was glad I had agreed to do the interview, and I enjoyed the experience. I also learned that sometimes you need to push yourself and try new things. Anthony and the marketing team had recognized my communication skills in PR training—they'd seen something in me that I didn't know existed. I was glad I went out on a limb and tried something new. Sometimes, you just need to say "yes."

Helping Others Out of Their Comfort Zones

Over the course of your career, you'll find dealing with your comfort zone is a persistent issue. But equally as persistent will be helping your colleagues and those you supervise out of *their* comfort zones.

I had the chance to offer a big promotion to a member of my team. This team member, Sandy, was a long-term successful manager and top performer.

An opportunity came for her to move into a regional VP role. I knew she would be a great candidate for the job. I reached out to her former boss to see what she thought about me approaching Sandy with the opportunity. While her former supervisor agreed with my assessment of Sandy's suitability, she told me that Sandy had repeatedly declined the additional responsibilities that came with this type of regional role for years. Over and over, Sandy kept declining additional responsibility.

Although Sandy had previously declined promotion opportunities, I decided to approach her directly to see what she thought. While I believed that she would be perfect for this opportunity, I realized there might be personal issues or other reasons holding her back.

Sandy and I had only recently started working together. She didn't know me very well, but we had worked at the same company for some time and we both knew each other's track record. I scheduled a time for us to talk on a video call to discuss the role.

We had a very open and honest discussion about what she wanted to do and the opportunity in front of her. We spoke for about an hour, and I could tell she was interested in a bigger role with more responsibility. But she still had some reservations about accepting a promotion.

"Joanie, I have two school-age kids," she said. "I'll be honest with you—they are my top priority. I'm interested in a bigger role, but I don't want to take it on if I'll be in over my head."

"I totally understand," I replied. "I have two kids too, and as a single parent, I completely understand being a mom comes first. Only you can decide if this new job is right for you or not."

As I think back to that meeting, I realized that there are several considerations when asking someone to assume a stretch role, promotion, or new assignment:

- Go to the source! Never let someone else speak for another. Always go directly to the person to find out if they would consider an opportunity, special project, or stretch assignment.

- Share your vision of how they fit into your organization and/or the job at hand. In Sandy's case, I wanted to paint a picture of how she would play an important leadership role in growing the company. I wanted to show her she would be a key member of the management team.
- Create confidence around their abilities and potential to assume the new role, assignment, or promotion. Highlight why you think they are ready. Point out their strengths and let them know you believe in them.
- Discuss tools, resources, and support that is available to position them for long-term success.
- Understand the personal dynamics and their situation. Do they have young children or an elderly or sick parent? Are they a single parent who needs flexibility? You must understand if there are dynamics holding them back from taking that next step. Even if there's a good reason, it's important to be on the same page.
- Offer time and space for the person to think and consider their options after you discuss the role, responsibilities, and why you think they should take on a stretch assignment.

I am happy to say that after Sandy and I discussed all these points, she decided she was ready to take that next step. She accepted the promotion and transitioned extremely well into her new responsibility. She was ready to take on that new assignment, spread her wings, and fly high. Sometimes, you just have to nudge someone along for them to take the leap. With Sandy, it was important for her to understand that there was a robust safety net supporting her, and that the confidence of management to succeed in this new role was solely behind her.

When to Say "No"

Don't get me wrong—I'm not advocating stretch assignments for everyone under every circumstance. In fact, there are times when taking a stretch assignment might not be the best decision. Even the most expertly laid out plans can fall through. In other cases, you might be stretching yourself too thin or have too much on your plate. It is important to make sure you have the bandwidth and support to be successful.

A few years back, I was running a division of my company. Overall, both the division and the company were well-positioned and performing at a high level. I was at a point where I knew I had some bandwidth. I wanted a bit more of a challenge.

The company's chief marketing officer had recently resigned. As a result, many of the marketing initiatives were struggling to gain traction. I've always enjoyed sales and marketing, so it seemed like the timing was right to stretch myself by lending a hand with marketing until a new CMO was in place.

When I offered my assistance, Tom (our CEO) was thrilled. He quickly took me up on my offer. I rolled up my sleeves and jumped into the marketing strategy. As I told him, "Let me help get things moving in the right direction. Then when you hire a CMO, I will turn the department over to them in a better position than we are in today."

When I dug into the actual work, I could clearly understand what needed to be done with the company's branding and messaging. But I also realized there was a problem. A big problem. The company had financial constraints to invest, and we didn't have the right technology stack in place to leverage new digital and marketing tools.

As time went on, Tom asked me to step in as the CMO while I was still running a line of business. Suddenly I had two big executive roles with the company, and I didn't have the funding to run marketing properly. In addition, the marketing team needed so much attention and work that I was spending all my time with them. This came as a huge detriment to my divisional responsibilities.

Before long, I realized I had made a mistake in committing to two full-time roles—neither of which allowed any room for error. Even working round-the-clock hours, I could not successfully juggle both positions. As time passed, I realized I was doing a disservice to my division, to the marketing team, my family, and myself. How could I succeed without the proper resources or investment for either position?

Though I had made some great progress with marketing strategy, branding, and public relations, I knew I didn't have the funding to set up the digital platform and technology necessary to make a significant difference. In addition, the business I was running was suffering and needed my attention and leadership. If I couldn't devote more time, the division would need a leader who could run it on a day-to-day basis.

I scheduled some time to talk with Tom about making changes. I was working around the clock and headed towards burnout if something didn't change. When I scheduled the meeting with him, he said he also needed to update me on a couple of changes he was making. I figured it was perfect timing to have an open and honest conversation.

"Tom, I've loved having a broader role on the leadership team and leading the marketing efforts for the company. But this is a full-time job, and I need to either be in marketing 100% of the time or go back to running my business line 100% of the time," I said.

"I agree, Joanie," he said, nodding. "You've done an amazing job of moving the needle for our messaging and branding. But I can see this is a big job that needs investment, which we aren't prepared to make right now. I also know your division is struggling and needs more of your time and attention."

"I appreciate that," I said. And I meant it.

"I want to let you know in confidence that I'm planning to retire," he said.

It was quite a revelation.

"Wow," I exclaimed. "I wasn't expecting you to say that."

"The board is in the final stages of looking for a new CEO," he confided. "Think about which role you'd prefer to stick with, since it isn't feasible for you to handle both positions. I'm confident you'll make the right choice for you and for the company."

This stretch assignment had been an incredible experience, and I was grateful for it—but the time had come to make a change. Over the next few weeks, I considered the pros and cons of both positions, finally deciding to remain as the head of my division. Though I loved the CMO role, and it was an incredible experience, I knew my goal was to run a larger business.

The Bottom Line

Stretch assignments help you gain knowledge and experience, both of which position you for future success. But it is critical to ensure you're ready to take them on. Before you accept a stretch assignment, make sure you have the right resources and support in place to set you up for a favorable outcome. Sometimes you need to take the leap and go for it—other times you may weigh your options and decide the timing isn't the best.

Looking back on my experience with Anthony, I am very glad I said "yes" to filling in for my previous CEO on TV. Following that first interview, the network called back and asked to book me again. Tig used to joke that I stole his spot on TV, but I truly believe he was happy to have someone else who could represent the company. I'm thankful I was given the opportunity and glad I had the confidence in myself to say "yes." In fact, that one "yes" eventually led to my speaking on Fox News, CNN, NBC, CNBC, and a regular role on the Fox Business Network. You never know where those stretch assignments might take you—but it sure can be fun seeing what doors may open.

CHAPTER SEVEN REFLECTION

One of the best ways to advance your learning and skills is by taking on stretch assignments. If you haven't taken advantage of these opportunities and you are ambitious to climb the ladder, then I suggest you ask yourself the following:

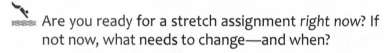 Are you ready for a stretch assignment *right now*? If not now, what needs to change—and when?

In what area(s) would you like to gain more experience or learn new skills?

What skills do you need to get you to that next promotion?

Who can you ask for advice and recommendations in order to achieve that next promotion?

STRATEGY 3

EXECUTE:
TAKE OFF & FLY HIGH

ABOVE THE LINE ACCOUNTABILITY

"Some people want it to happen, some wish it would happen, others make it happen."
– Michael Jordan

As an ambitious and motivated employee, I was always on the lookout for advice. Early in my career, I was fortunate enough to meet James, a very successful entrepreneur. James also happened to be an investor and advisor to the company I worked for at the time, and he took me under his wing for a few years. Through my friendship with James, I learned a great deal about how to create a unique value proposition for a business and how to back it up with strategies and marketing.

"Joanie," James said one day after a meeting about the company's marketing strategy. "Have I ever told you about my take on the lifeline?"

"No," I said curiously, shaking my head.

"It's something I learned about at a workshop," he said enthusiastically. "It changed my life and the way I approach business. Let me show you." He took out some markers and started to write on a white board. "You always want to put yourself in a powerful position. To do that, you've got to live your life above the line."

He drew a horizontal line in the middle of the white board, then continued, "That means you do the following things: number one: be accountable by owning your actions. Number two: acknowledge reality. Number three: no excuses. Number four: find solutions. Number five: make it happen." He wrote these phrases above the line, then pointed at them for emphasis. "This is where you want to stay."

Starting to write below the line, he continued, "People who live below the line tend to act like victims, putting themselves in a weak position. How? Number one: by blaming others. Number two: making excuses. Number three: they say they can't execute. Number four: waiting and hoping things improve. Finally, they either quit or give up." As he talked, he wrote those phrases below the line.

"Think about it this way," he said. "Someone who lives below the line and who says they want to quit smoking will make excuses for why they can't. Or they'll blame other people or say they just can't stop. Essentially, they are acting like a victim and creating space for failure instead of success. In a way, they are burying themselves in the ground, and there's no way out because of their consistently negative behavior."

I had never heard these powerful ideas presented in quite this way.

"Now, when you think about someone who lives above the line—someone who wants to quit smoking, for example— they will own their behavior. Instead of creating space for failure, they will create space for success," James said. "They own the problem, accept reality, make plans to quit, and then stick with it. If they encounter barriers, they find ways around them. They don't whine. They don't complain. Ultimately, they demonstrate power and accountability."

James told me how much adopting this philosophy had changed his life. That resonated with me—not only because I respected him, but also because my parents had raised my sisters and me that way. I consider myself a person who strives to live their life above the line. While I've made many mistakes and poor choices, I own my failures just as I own my successes. I don't blame others when things happen to me. When I face adversity, I accept the reality of a situation. I try to find solutions to fix it.

Throughout my childhood, my parents taught my sisters and me that if we wanted something, we had to put in the effort to achieve it. We were raised to tell the truth and to never blame others. Most of all, we were taught never to give up or quit.

After decades as a manager and executive, I must say that one of the traits that is most indicative of whether someone will succeed or not in any given role is whether they live above or below the line. Really, there's nothing that frustrates me more than individuals who play the victim in work and in life. There's no room for the victim persona on my team.

Living the Lifeline at Work

Over the years, I have had many of what I call "lifeline conversations" with employees. One incident that sticks out is a coaching conversation I had with one of my team leaders, Steven, on how to create more accountability within his team. I could see that while Steven had a tremendous amount of potential, he was struggling as a manager. He was trying to make everyone happy instead of offering constructive feedback, engaging in difficult conversations, and confronting his team members.

All that was difficult enough, but what really concerned me was his propensity to blame others, make up his own rules, and fail to create consistent processes. To me, his behavior clearly fell below the line. His negative traits were not only impacting his own functionality, but also the success of his entire team.

It was time for the lifeline conversation. Not only would I relate the story to Steven, but I also decided *he* would present it *to his team* as a springboard to improve their performance and get back on track.

As I walked into the conference room where we were meeting, I was happy to see a white board. With it, I could drive home the lesson by drawing the same illustration that James had used with me all those years ago. Having this conversation in person is great because you can see when something clicks. I described the attributes to living above the line and watched as Steven agreed and nodded his head.

"Makes sense," he said.

Then I started to describe the below the line behaviors. His eyes widened, and his body language seemed deflated. The lightbulb moment had come: Steven recognized that sometimes he was falling below the line by blaming others or coming up with excuses.

He turned to me and said, "Joanie, I never really thought about it this way, but you are right. There are times when I blame other people instead of owning the problem or challenge. In fact, my team does it too. Sometimes it's easy to talk about what others are doing wrong instead of discussing what we could do differently."

I told him that it's normal for all of us to fall below the line at certain times. It happens to the best of us, including me. The key is to recognize it, stop acting like a victim, and reverse the behavior.

"Steven, think about how powerful it would be for you and your team to own the problem and find a solution," I said.

"I absolutely agree. 100 percent."

"Remember the time you came into my office to discuss a challenge you were having with employee turnover?" I asked.

"Yes."

"You recognized you had an employee who was a great producer, and you promoted them to management," I continued. "Joe was an outstanding employee, but he struggled managing other people. You realized Joe couldn't manage, motivate, or retain the employees in the department. In fact, you said you had made a mistake promoting Joe. You also came to me with a plan to make a change and options to move him back to a producing role. We discussed it and I agreed with your solution."

"That was a tough one," he agreed.

"It was a perfect example of how you put yourself in a powerful and accountable position. You acknowledged the reality, owned the problem, found a solution, and made things happen. I was very impressed with how you proactively took responsibility and returned Joe to his producer role without blaming him for his failure as a manager."

"Thanks, Joanie!" Steven said. He sat up straighter, looking proud of how he had handled that situation. "I really appreciate you sharing the lifeline concept with me," he continued. "I'm going to have this lifeline talk with my team this week. I think we all know how to live above the line. We may have fallen off the tracks at times, but we will get back."

Smiling, I said, "I have no doubt. Let me know how I can support you and your team."

In the ensuing weeks and months, I noticed big changes from Steven and his team. They were committed to acknowledging reality, owning it, finding solutions, and making it happen. They stopped blaming other departments and making excuses. There was a paradigm shift in the way they thought about their business. They continued to improve and perform extremely well.

A few years later, Steven and his team achieved Presidents Club, an annual awards trip for outstanding performance and growth. They had put themselves into a powerful and accountable position. They owned their success, and they made it happen.

Living Above the Line at Home

Sometimes we need to make that paradigm shift in our personal lives. Have we neglected taking care of ourselves? Do we need to lose a few pounds? Quit smoking? Are we in an unhealthy relationship? What is the reality of the situation? It can be difficult to admit you've been living below the line. But you need to look yourself in the mirror and acknowledge your reality.

One of my most difficult personal experiences of acknowledging reality was being in an unhealthy relationship and not doing anything about it. I kept telling myself I could fix the situation. I expected things to improve over time. I ignored the reality instead of acknowledging the truth. Living below the line at home led me to not only lose joy and happiness in my life, but also blame my partner for taking it away from me. This had to stop. I was in denial about the challenges and issues we faced. Denial can be very powerful, and it might seem easier to do nothing. Facing and accepting reality means having to work hard to find solutions and fix things. It can also mean making some difficult and painful changes.

I decided to speak to a therapist to help me sort out my feelings and properly approach the situation. One day, I was sitting in her office when something clicked. I thought of the lifeline, and how I needed to put myself in a powerful position. I had to acknowledge the reality of the relationship. I needed to own up to the situation and how I was enabling the behavior. I had to set some boundaries of what was acceptable and what wasn't—no excuses. I was committed to finding solutions. This also meant couples therapy—a lot of it. Together, we tried to find solutions, and we started to communicate much better. Though we made progress, the relationship was sadly beyond repair. We acknowledged the reality of the situation and realized we saw things differently. We also had different priorities and values. We had to own up to our own issues and not blame one another. Finding the solution meant we agreed to separate. I wish it had a better ending, but unfortunately it didn't.

Though the relationship ended, it was the right decision. It ultimately led to a much happier and peaceful life. If I had stayed below the line, I would have acted as a victim, which would have led to a miserable life. Ultimately, I would rather live my life above the line. I aim to surround myself with people who live the same way.

Living Above the Line at Scale

I've run a business for the last seven years. When I first started with the company, I noticed there was a bit more below the line behavior than I wanted to see: for example, people blaming each other and making excuses for why they weren't performing.

Walking through the office, I would overhear conversations along the lines of: "Well, if we had better technology or if our credit team wasn't so strict with terms and conditions, I could bring that new customer in." Pointing fingers was a real habit. Obviously, this behavior wasn't going to fly with me. Working under my leadership, you need to live above the line. I don't accept people blaming others, making excuses, or acting as a victim. You can't wait around or hope things might get better.

I started to introduce the concept of living above the line in our leadership meetings. The team embraced the philosophy, and they used it with their employees.

Today, we've established a culture of accountability and delivering results. In fact, we are celebrating another record year of double-digit growth in revenue and profits. Sustainable results can't be achieved without creating a culture of accountability. My team finds solutions and they make things happen. They live above the line, and it shows. I couldn't be prouder or more grateful for their hard work and commitment.

The Value of Experience & Perspective

There may be instances throughout your career when you disagree with your superior or your company's strategy. You might also work for someone or a company that doesn't align with your values and priorities. Most of us experience this at some point in our career. Your inclination may be to jump ship. If you find yourself in this situation, take some time to see how it unfolds. Don't rush into quitting or looking for a new job before you give it some time. On more than one occasion, I have seen poor leaders work themselves out of their job. You might end up with a new boss who you love. It has certainly happened to me.

I once worked for a gentleman who was a very intelligent person. But sadly, he was also a micromanager and a terrible leader. I knew he would not be successful in his role if he didn't change his leadership style. It didn't take long for others to see he was struggling in his position and couldn't connect with people. He was difficult to work for, and I wasn't motivated by his management style.

I didn't want to leave my job, so I decided to give the situation some time and to try my best to make it work over the next six months. Then at the end of that period, I would reassess if things were improving or not. During that time, I resolved not to complain. Instead, I would try to handle the situation with grace and grit. I would be respectful to him but also go above and beyond to meet my objectives. I would confront him in areas where we had differences of opinion, but I would lead with facts and data. And I would always handle conversations respectfully. I didn't like or agree with his abrasive and demanding style, but I could handle it. Lucky for me, he was let go before those six months ended. And what happened? I ended up with a wonderful new boss who created an amazing working environment. I was grateful I hadn't rushed into a decision to leave and that I'd stayed respectful in my interactions with my former boss.

Of course, there will be times when things don't work out in such an ideal manner. A point may come where you need to make a change. We have all heard the saying, "Never burn a bridge." That is good advice to follow when it comes to quitting a job. I have had to coach many candidates through the resignation process. Believe me, I understand you might want to take the opportunity to tell your boss how you really feel about them, the company, or the work environment. But I wouldn't recommend it.

The best advice I can give is to handle the situation with the utmost professionalism. Thank your employer for the opportunity. Let them know you have decided to make a change. Tell them you have been offered a position elsewhere and have accepted a new role. You should also offer to provide a two-weeks' notice to smoothly transition your responsibilities to others. Most importantly, hold your head high. Don't give anyone a reason to say a bad thing about you. Here's why:

- It's a small world. You never know when and where your paths might cross again. Your boss could also make a change someday, and you could both end up working at the same place again.
- Your new company could acquire your old employer, or your old employer could acquire your new employer. It happens. I have firsthand experience of this happening.
- You might end up disliking your new job and wish you were back at your old employer.
- Your new employer could face tough times and be forced to downsize.
- You want to build connections in your field and be remembered for handling things as a true professional.

Always leave a job, assignment, company, or boss on good terms. It is wise to leave the door—or at least a window—open. Take the high road whenever possible and always make a graceful exit.

Whether you're dealing with personal or business situations, the bottom-line rules must establish accountability, responsibility, and clear communication around the reality of the situation. There's no future in blaming others. If you want to succeed in life, you need to take responsibility, find solutions, stay accountable, and make it happen. Live above the line.

CHAPTER EIGHT REFLECTION

Accountability is one of the most important characteristics of high-performing and successful people. A lack of accountability, on the other hand, can keep you from reaching your full potential. Accountability in the workplace and in life means taking responsibility for your performance and the outcomes. Instead of playing the "blame game" when something goes awry, you step up and take full ownership. You work to find solutions. As a result, you will thrive.

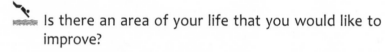 Is there an area of your life that you would like to improve?

 Where might you be living above or below the line?

What can you do to find solutions to obstacles or challenges that may be holding you back?

What steps or actions do you need to take to put yourself in a powerful and accountable position?

ALL-OUT EFFORT

"I am a great believer in luck, and I find the harder I work, the more I have of it."
– Thomas Jefferson

In 1999, I attended a company leadership meeting in Orlando. I was 28 years old and had recently achieved my goal of becoming a vice president with my firm.

One of the highlights of the trip was a dinner in Disney's Hall of Presidents, followed by fireworks from the steamboats—all at the Disney World Complex. I hadn't been to Disney since going on a family vacation with my parents and sisters 15 years prior, which was one of my most cherished memories. In fact, Disney was one of my favorite places—anywhere.

Just when I thought the trip couldn't get any better, the room quieted down as Tom, the company president, got up to say a few words. He was preparing to give out the awards for the previous year's top performers.

As his assistant handed him the envelope to open, Tom said, "The individuals I'm about to recognize have produced the top results in terms of revenue growth, gross profit growth, EBITDA growth, and highest employee retention."

A buzz arose from the tables as we waited to hear the results. My peers were a mix of male and female leaders ranging in age from 30 to 50. Looking at the organization, I estimated there were about 25 of us in the same position across the country. Each of us possessed different specialties and geographies, but we didn't have much insight into one another's performance. Because the organization didn't share financial performance across the organization, it was hard for me to know where I ranked relative to others in my position.

Beginning from the fifth-place spot, the CEO began to read the names. As he continued to work his way through the announcement, I was curious as to who would be number one. Would it be Gary, or maybe Carolyn? Both were long-time VPs with impressive track records. They were role models I looked up to and admired.

For the second-place award, our CEO recognized one of my peers whose work history I was familiar with. We were in the same division. Our results were always neck-and-neck.

Suddenly, I realized I had a shot at winning. Not only winning VP of the Year—but at becoming the youngest of the whole group to sweep all categories and receive the award.

I sat up straight in my chair, listening intently as Tom spoke about the top VP. He was boasting about their growth in all categories and highlighting their record in employee retention.

Then he said it: "Joanie!"

To say I was shocked would be an understatement. I'd had absolutely no idea that my performance would rank as the best overall for 1999.

As I walked towards Tom, I couldn't stop smiling.

Shaking my hand, he presented me with a beautiful crystal trophy from Tiffany's (which I still treasure today) and a check. Funny thing is, the check didn't mean nearly as much as the recognition and the knowledge that my team had achieved the best results in the company.

Standing in the Hall of Presidents at Disney and being recognized as a top performer in the company was a moment I will always treasure. I was honored and humbled. And of course, I had to go call my parents as soon as I got the chance.

One of my role models, Carolyn, couldn't have been more supportive and thoughtful about my award. She instilled in me a sense of worthiness. I will always be grateful for her kindness and generosity.

Something else about that night stands out to me. A male colleague twice my age approached me and said, "Joanie, congratulations. Very impressive. But you know, as well deserved as this award is, what would be impressive is if you could pull it off two years in a row."

Now, I consider myself a smart girl. I can read people's body language and interpret the true meaning behind their words. To me, what this male colleague had really said was, "You got lucky this year. If you're *actually* good, let's see you do it again."

I could be wrong, but it seemed he was a bit jealous of my recognition. Little did he know he was only providing me with adversity—fueling my drive and passion to show him he was wrong about my "luck."

Throughout my career, I've always been the type of person to keep my head down and give the work my best effort. I believed my performance and results would stand for themselves and get me noticed for advancement opportunities if I gave it my best. It doesn't always work that way, but some things are out of our control.

Putting in your best effort means you give it your all. In sports they say, 'leave it all on the field'. If you ever took an Orangetheory Fitness class you would be familiar with the terms: base, push, and all-out. All-out is the fastest pace you can run on the treadmill. When you're working hard, you give it everything you've got and go all-out. To perform at work and in life, we must give our best efforts. I always encourage others to do their best work and give their best efforts because they are worth it.

The Backstory

When I was a teenager, my parents told me that if I wanted a car, I needed to get a job and save up my money. They generously told me they would match whatever I saved to help me purchase my first car, but I'm not sure they realized how motivated I was. I applied for a job at Sears Roebuck and soon after was offered a position as a cashier in the hardware department. I signed up for as many hours as I could possibly work. I was just barely making over minimum wage, but I was thrilled. I saved every paycheck and worked toward building my bank account.

The manager of the department was an older gentleman, Harvey. He was sweet as can be. I also worked in the department with a bunch of other men who worked on commission. This was their full-time job, and I could see they were very competitive with one another. This was my first taste of sales and business. Looking back, I know I learned a lot working at Sears in the late 1980s.

One day, when Harvey was reviewing the previous day's sales reports, I asked him to explain what the reports were and what exactly they tracked. Curious and ambitious to make more money to buy my own car, I was interested in moving into a role where I could earn commissions.

"Harvey," I said. "What would it take for me to be promoted into a commissioned sales role?"

"Joanie, everyone selling tools, lawn equipment, patio furniture, and gas grills are men," he said, chuckling. "This is their full-time job. They know the merchandise and how to sell it."

"Okay," I said. "Could I shadow some of them to learn about the equipment and how to sell it? And then maybe if a sales opportunity opens up, I might be ready to take it on?"

He thought about it for a few minutes. He knew just as well as I did that there were plenty of quiet weekday nights when the department was empty of customers, and all the employees stood around chatting. I figured this would be a good opportunity for me to learn.

"Okay, Joanie," he said.

I could see that he thought he was just indulging a teenager's whim, a girl who would soon be bored and move on. But I was determined. I would immerse myself in learning all about weed whackers and BTUs on gas grills. I spent every free moment asking questions and learning about the different products. I gave my best effort to learn all I could. The guys appreciated my interest and enjoyed sharing their knowledge with me (up until a point). Finally, I was asked to work on commission one day for a big sale.

"I'm going to give you a chance to work the Labor Day sales weekend on commission," Harvey said. "Are you up for the challenge?"

"Yes!"

I was ecstatic, thinking to myself: *Are you kidding?* Of course, I was up for the challenge. This was the big break I'd been seeking. Though only a junior in high school, I was determined to climb the ladder and make more money to buy that first car.

I worked all weekend long. I put in as many hours as I could. Needless to say, it was a great sales weekend. The guys in the department didn't say too much. I think at the time they were glad to have the help so they could enjoy some of the holiday weekend with their families.

"Joanie!" Harvey called out across the department the Tuesday after Labor Day. "Come into my office! I want to show you the sales reports!"

I ran into his office, thrilled to discover that I was one of the top salespeople. I was so excited to get my first commission check that next week. Everyone was happy, and I was getting closer to that car.

As time went on, I got better and better at dealing with customers and more confident in my knowledge of the products. However, I could sense that my colleagues weren't as friendly anymore. I was starting to outperform their numbers, and customers liked dealing with me. At least Harvey was thrilled with my performance. He was glad to have my work ethic in the department.

One day, during a busy weekend sale, I was ringing up a customer's purchases at the register. Out of nowhere, one of the older gentlemen in the department came up to the customer and took their purchases out of their hands. He pushed me out of the way of the register.

"I got this, Joanie. I'll ring it up," Kevin said.

He literally pushed me out of the way and took the sale over. He may have been twice my age, but I wasn't scared. This was not how we worked. I let him ring the customer up, and when the customer left, I confronted him.

"What you did was off limits, Kevin. Why did you do that?" I asked. I was furious.

"Hey, this is my job!" he replied. "You can't step in here and try to take over."

I realized he was frustrated that I—a high school student— was outperforming him. However, I was doing it honestly, by outworking him. Put simply: I was friendlier with customers than he was, and they liked dealing with me. I was helpful and knowledgeable on the products, and I was working my butt off to do the best job I could.

This was the business of sales. This was competition. This was also my first taste of adversity in the workplace, and likely a bit of gender discrimination as well. However, I decided I wasn't going to let him—or anyone—get to me. I was going to stand my ground, hold my head high, and not let him walk all over me. And that's exactly what I did.

I could have quit, gone crying to Harvey, or filed a complaint. But I didn't. I decided to put my head down, do my job, and do the best I could. I wasn't raised to complain or cry. I was raised to be confident in my abilities. I was raised to be honest and work hard.

In the end, I was highly successful at Sears. The job and opportunity enabled me to save enough money to buy my first car. More importantly, I learned some new skills that helped prepare me for today.

Dealing with Adversity

Adversity is part of life—something you'll absolutely have to deal with at some point. I've learned a three-step process for dealing with the inevitable adversity that arises on the job:

1. Stay confident in yourself and your beliefs. Always do your best and advocate for yourself and others.
2. Be knowledgeable and prepared. Be the expert of your domain. Put in the effort—no shortcuts.
3. Focus on what you can control, including your temperament. Don't let others get the best of you. Stay calm and carry on.

As for the gentleman who came up to me in Disney in 1999: I am thankful for him. Whether he meant to or not, he inspired me to put my head down and do the best I could in 2000 so I could win the top spot again—which I did.

Regardless of your role and your specific responsibilities, focusing on what you can control is important. You can use outside forces to motivate or threaten you, but you need to keep focused on the tasks at hand.

One day, at Orangetheory Fitness the coach belted out a quote that I love: "Hard work beats talent when talent fails to work hard." I looked up the quote when I got back home and saw that the phrase was first coined by high school basketball coach Tim Notke and made popular by a few famous athletes as well. This quote resonated with me. Maybe we aren't the smartest, most talented, or most skilled in a certain area, but you can't take away work ethic and effort.

I have seen these same characteristics in my children when they want to do well. One summer, my son worked on his golf game every single day, even amid challenging conditions of summer heat and storms. He wanted to make the varsity team, so he practiced constantly. He spent hours on the range, playing rounds of golf daily. He worked on his chipping and his putting consistently. He would arrive home drenched in sweat, take a shower, change his clothes, eat dinner, and then head back out to practice again. That year, he started the golf season on varsity. He also competed in a state golf tournament and took first place. His hard work and dedication helped him beat out talent on his team and nationally ranked players from Florida. He put in his best effort and outworked others.

Now, there have been other times when he didn't put in the time or hard work. Unsurprisingly, he didn't perform as well those times. He knows if he doesn't practice and put in the effort, he will struggle in golf—and in life.

My daughter is similar with dance. She will practice a routine over and over to perfect her technique for a performance. She will spend countless hours rehearsing and watching videos of herself and her team. She is committed to putting in the effort and hard work to be successful. She is also the same way with her studies, and it shows in her impressive grades. I couldn't be a prouder parent, especially when they are working towards achieving their goals and passions in life. They have both learned the lesson that hard work pays off and you should always give your best effort.

I use the example of my children because I believe work ethic is a foundational building block—one we all must learn at some point in our lives. When you put in the effort, commitment, dedication, and time, you can achieve great things. I try to lead by example for my children, and I hope they carry these traits into their professional and adult lives. They will need them. We all need them. We are not entitled to anything. If you want to succeed in life, you need to put in the hard work to make it happen.

This past year, my company held its Presidents Club award trip in Cabo San Lucas. As the president of my division, I am fortunate to attend this event to host my employees who achieved Presidents Club status. The company does a phenomenal job of recognizing and celebrating our top performers. One of the things I love most about this trip is that our employees are recognized as the best of the best in front of their significant others. Our employees work so hard, and this is an opportunity to celebrate their efforts and achievements.

Throughout the year, the employees are ranked based on their contributions, and they strive to be at the top of the list to win this award and the well-deserved recognition that comes along with it. It's a robust competition that is not easy to win, but I will say that every year it is interesting to see a consistent group of achievers win the award. When I look at the consistent group of award winners, I can clearly identify common traits. And I assure you it is not luck. These winners are goal-oriented. They set new targets every year and they put in the planning, hard work, and their best effort to achieve their goals. They track their progress, they know their numbers, and they know what they need to do to achieve their desired results. Their hard work pays off.

I had a very special surprise at the event last year. I was recognized by my wonderful boss, Steve, and our new CEO, Billy, as the Leader of the Year. This award is given to a leader who demonstrates growth and profitability, and who builds a successful business with a positive culture. My team had delivered exceptional growth over the past few years, and I was honored to receive the award for all our efforts. We had a record-breaking year, and we had worked hard as a team to accomplish our goals and objectives. But most of all, I was proud of the culture and environment we created. Not only were we recognized for our financial results, but we were recognized for building an engaged workforce that was accomplishing some incredible things year after year. It's not luck. It's a process and it takes all-out effort. Goal setting works—but you must work hard to make it happen. Hard work and giving your best effort are key to achieving goals and successful results.

A special note to share. The Leader of the Year Award is named after Chip Grissom. Chip was a well-loved, successful, and accomplished leader in the staffing industry. Sadly, he lost his battle to cancer shortly after I joined EmployBridge. The award is engraved with these words:

Face your reality. Don't give in to your emotions. Keep it simple. Control your attitude. Keep your support group intact. Whatever your faith, tap into it. Never give in. Never give up. – Chip Grissom

CHAPTER NINE REFLECTION

Developing a rigorous work ethic is directly proportional to building a successful career and life, and it often paves the way for interesting and challenging opportunities. Working hard influences your daily decision-making and allows you to create strong values that eventually go on to define you as an individual. Having a strong work ethic offers you a host of advantages, including improved job performance, higher job satisfaction, career advancement, and a brighter future both in and out of work.

Are there areas of your career or life that you need to put more effort into?

Are you putting in the effort and hard work to perform at your best?

What areas or skills do you need to practice more?

What effort do you need to achieve the next level? What specifically will it take?

What things have you procrastinated doing? What is your plan to get them accomplished?

BRAND YOU

*"You never get a second chance to
make a first impression."*
– Will Rogers

"What should I wear?" my client, Lindsay, asked me. She was preparing for an interview, and I could tell she was nervous.

"Wear your best dress to impress the hiring manager," I suggested. I'm a big believer in dressing to impress, and I always take the time to help my candidates prepare for an interview. Preparation for any meeting—especially an interview—is key to a successful outcome.

"Make sure you always make a good first impression," I said encouragingly. "You want to put your best foot forward and find a way to stand out from a crowd." This was my advice to many candidates preparing for a first interview. By following this advice, they can feel more confident, make a good impression, and be remembered for looking sharp.

"Okay," Lindsay said quietly. She was clearly doubting herself a bit.

"You'll do great," I said.

The next day, just as I was wondering how Lindsay's interview was going, my phone rang.

"Uh, Joanie, this is Tim, the hiring manager."

"Yes, Tim! Is there a problem?" I said, looking at the clock. The interview with Lindsay was starting any minute.

"Well," Tim said, clearing his throat, "when I went down to bring Lindsay up for the interview, I looked through the glass wall and saw she was sitting there in, um ..."

"In what?" I asked. Now I was alarmed.

"Well, I'm not sure," he said apologetically. "My assistant thinks it's a prom dress."

"WHAT?" I said, stunned. This was a new one for me.

"I'm going to get her now, but I just wanted you to know," he said as he tried not to break out in laughter.

"Uh, thanks," I said as he hung up the phone.

I put my head in my hands, unsure of whether to laugh or cry. I didn't think Lindsay would be getting the job. And she didn't.

This situation happened early in my career. After that little incident, I was much more specific with my candidates about what their best dress or best suit meant. I didn't want someone else showing up in a wedding dress, a tuxedo, or a bathing suit.

First Impressions Count

There's an old saying: You only have one chance to make that first impression. Though there is some truth to that saying, social media gives us a chance to make many impressions on different audiences. In today's world, your social media presence may precede your first in-person impression. That is why it is so important to build and protect a professional online presence.

Through social channels, we can connect with friends, family, and colleagues, sharing what we consider appropriate. There's no doubt that social media has revolutionized society. You probably have your own opinions about whether those changes are positive or negative. Regardless of which way you slice it, the world with social media is far different than the world before social media. Today, you can connect with virtually anyone instantaneously, sharing stories, photos, and life experiences through hundreds of different avenues. As you engage in this process, you're building a brand, reputation, and online identity—whether you think about it that way or not.

Once you enter the online universe, you're essentially living in a fishbowl. Your friends, family, colleagues, and even people you don't know or have never met can find out almost anything about you at any time. So, it's critical to intentionally build an appropriate professional reputation online. Protect yourself by being careful with what you share regarding your personal life, likes, dislikes, hobbies, and so forth.

Regardless of whether you are a plumber, teacher, salesperson, doctor, or CEO, your reputation and online brand will create an impression. That impression ultimately will impact your success and ability to position yourself as an expert in your field. Before social media, you might have been able to get away with a few hand-selected references to vouch for your work. But today, there's a whole online world with reputation reviews, comments, and ratings that will speak for you. The landscape of online references and reviews is evolving rapidly and applies to businesses and individuals—including you. You don't have to take my word for it, just look at the recommendations on LinkedIn or the influencers on Instagram.

Social Media and Recruiting

Just a few decades ago, the best way to find a job was to search the help wanted ads in the newspaper, then write a cover letter and enclose that with a resume. Finally, you would send that enclosed parcel to the hiring manager through what we would today call "snail mail."

But the advent of the internet has changed the hiring landscape through online job boards, social media sites, and online recruiting. Today, employers can search for candidates through social media platforms, buy targeted job advertising for specific demographics, and more. As this phenomenon further evolves, employers will continue to access additional methods to find and recruit top talent.

While there's no way to know exactly what social media platforms of the future will look like or how they will impact the recruiting process, there's a lot that we know about this landscape in 2022 and 2023 (the time of my writing this book). Here are some statistics to get you thinking:

- Social and professional networks were the #1 method employers used to recruit talent in 2021, with 92% saying they used social media and professional networks for recruiting.[25]
- Social media and social media recruiting software top the list of top technology investments for recruiters, with 41% saying they increased their investment in 2021.[26]

- 89% of employers are recruiting virtually (but only 19% favor virtual recruiting over in-person recruiting).[27]
- 61% of recruiters surveyed by Jobvite believe that the hiring process in the future will be a combination of virtual and in person.[28]
- More than two-thirds of recruiters surveyed by Jobvite use Facebook and LinkedIn for job recruiting.[29]

Clearly, building a positive personal and professional brand has never been more important. You have a choice about which platforms to leverage and to what degree you want to build your online brand and reputation. You could choose to engage with platforms like LinkedIn, Instagram, Twitter, TikTok, and Facebook (to name a few). Through these sites, you can present yourself, your expertise, your thoughts, and your opinions. You can share content and express yourselves to the world if you choose. At the same time, you can also ruin your personal brand if you make a wrong turn.

Here are a few things you should consider doing to boost your professional online profile. First and foremost, make sure you have an updated and accurate LinkedIn profile. This should include an accurate job history, awards, recognitions, and education. Second, connect with school alumni and others from your professional networks. Make sure you leverage social online profile sites to share relevant content to your field of study or work interest. A great way to position yourself as an expert is to share relative articles, research, and interesting facts related to the type of work you do and the expertise that you are developing.

Leveraging Social Media in Your Employer Research

Social media isn't just a one-way street. You, as a job candidate, can do far more to find open jobs and research potential employers, hiring managers, future bosses, and potential colleagues through social media and networking platforms. In fact, 73 percent of job seekers between the ages of 18 and 34 found their last job through a social media platform, and 86 percent of job seekers use social media in their job search. I recommend you follow the companies you are interested in working with on their major channels, which may not always intersect with your preferences. However, many employers—apart from some very small companies—will have a company LinkedIn page that will display employees who work for their company.

LinkedIn is a great place to start in terms of research when applying and interviewing. From an organizational LinkedIn page, you can easily find the company's website, social channels, and other information about specific divisions, departments, and affiliates. Before you have an initial interview, you'll want to gather specific information about the department or division you'd be working for, their current priorities, and past accomplishments. Many organizations frequently update their LinkedIn profile with news and media coverage. You should also be able to find more information through googling the company and consulting their website.

As you conduct research, jot down some questions to ask the hiring manager. It's far better to come prepared with questions—even if you end up asking different ones because of the information you gain in an interview— than to come with no questions at all. Curious candidates make a better impression than candidates who don't ask questions. They seem more involved and invested. If you can't think of questions, here are a few I recommend:

- What are the day-to-day responsibilities of this role?
- What are the opportunities for advancement in this role?

- What does success look like in the context of this role?
- How is performance measured in the department? How is feedback provided on that performance?
- What other roles/departments am I most likely to interact with in this role?
- What are the biggest challenges involved in this role?

If you learn the hiring manager's name in advance of the interview, or if you advance to a stage where you will be meeting with your potential boss, you may wonder how much digging you should do. That's a great question. While you want to be informed, you don't want to seem creepy. Obviously, if you and one of your interviewers share an alma mater, mention that. It's also helpful to know about the interviewers' backgrounds, job histories, and other professional information. But you want to be careful about crossing the line. Don't bring up personal information that you discovered through publicly available information on someone's Instagram, Snapchat, TikTok, or Facebook profile. After all, there will be plenty of time to learn more about your boss and co-workers once you get hired.

Impact of Upping Your Brand

It's more important now than ever before to have a professional online profile and presence. Not only that, but you must carefully and judiciously protect your personal brand and online presence to ensure that it will support your brand and reputation, not undermine them. In a recent survey by The Harris Poll, 70 percent of the employers who responded said they believe every company should screen candidates' social media profiles during the hiring process. Hiring managers are focused on recruiting the best possible talent to fit in with their organizations. That means they will thoroughly vet candidates, including their social media profiles, to make sure they hire those with appropriate online profiles and a good reputation.

As you build your brand, I would recommend you follow what I call the Seven Cs:

1. **Commitment**: Commit to building your brand. This requires planning and dedication. You don't have to be famous or even *want to* be famous. Make the commitment and effort to build brand "YOU." You are worth the investment.
2. **Creation**: What value creation are you bringing to an environment or situation? What can you offer? What are you passionate about? Whether you are Martha Stewart or Bill Nye the Science Guy, you need to share your passion with others and let it shine through.
3. **Clarity**: What is your message? How do you differentiate that message and your brand from others? What sets you apart from your peers and offers you an edge in today's marketplace? If you don't know, or if you feel like you don't have something that differentiates you, then you need to create it and find that edge. Be clear about who you are. Understanding what makes you authentic ties into the value you bring to the table and emphasizes your uniqueness, which is very important.
4. **Character**: What is your reputation? What are you known for and what do you want to be known for?
5. **Content**: Relevant content is king when it comes to building your brand. Write your own articles or share articles that are related to your field. Share them on LinkedIn or other social media sites.
6. **Consistency**: Are you consistent in your approach or erratic? It's important to post content consistently. You want to build a brand that people can count on.

7. **Community:** Define your audience. Focus on building your network. Don't be shy. To build a successful brand, you need to put yourself out there and promote yourself in a positive way. However, there is a fine line between self-promotion and bragging. Be careful to do it appropriately and humbly.

The Seven Cs are something you can build over time. But you need to spend time planning, writing, and refining them to help you build your best brand.

Years ago, I decided to study employment economic data and trends. Even though I don't have a business degree, I was fascinated about what was happening in employment. I started to read and subscribe to different business publications that covered employee and employer trends. I wanted to know what was motivating workers to stay or leave their employers, what steps employers could take to retain their workers, and how employers could maximize employee productivity and longevity. As I continued to research these topics, I grew fascinated, itching to learn more. Before long, I was using what I learned to enhance my understanding of the job market and employment trends, helping me offer the latest and greatest insights to my clients.

What started as an interest led me to carve out a niche for myself as a thought leader on workforce trends. My clients began approaching me when they needed advice or insight on the latest wage information, supply and demand data, or employment challenges. As I received more and more inquiries about labor market challenges, I realized that I was differentiating myself from my competition and building a reputation as a go-to resource on the latest employment trends and data. My customers perceived me as knowledgeable and competent—a trusted source of valuable insights. Before long, I was asked to host webinars and give presentations on current and future employment trends. I was even asked to speak at conferences and share my insights. I was becoming known as an employment expert while simultaneously building a strong brand and reputation in my industry.

The next step happened almost before I realized it. I was regularly asked to speak on national news programs and at industry events to discuss employment and workforce trends. My success emanated because I was diligently following the Seven Cs of Branding.

Recently, I decided to up my own brand persona by referring to myself as "The Duchess of Labor." I credit my very creative and intelligent daughter Ashley, for coming up with the name and logo. She had been learning about the Knights of Labor movement in the United States in her history class, a group focused on equity, health, and safety standards, and ending child labor. In fact, in 1881, the Knights of Labor declared that women be accepted as members and have equal rights. In many ways, this group was way ahead of its time.

My daughter and I discussed the Knights of Labor, unions, labor laws, and the fact that much work still needs to be done around diversity, equity, and inclusion today. She knows how strongly I believe in equality and opportunity for all genders and races. I want to see people thriving and participating in the workforce. So, knowing how passionate I am about this subject, and hearing me speak about the issue at home, at work, and on the national news, she jokingly referred to me as the "Duchess of Labor" one night at the dinner table. And I loved it.

I said to her, "I'm going to use that title and do something with it."

I registered duchessoflabor.com that evening, and a year later, she started helping me build the brand.

My efforts and energies create value for me in the industry and for my employer. I amplify my employer's brand by improving their reputation as a thought leader. My company values me as an extension of the brand and as a spokesperson. Plus, they receive free public relations and advertising every time I speak on National TV or at an industry event. A winning proposition for both of us.

CHAPTER TEN REFLECTION

In today's digital world, the hiring landscape has changed. It now relies more and more on social media sites, online job boards, and online recruiting. Employers can, and do, search for candidates through social media platforms and social networking. As this phenomenon will likely continue to grow, it's more important than ever before to have a professional online profile and build a brand presence. In addition, you must carefully and judiciously protect your personal brand and online presence to ensure it supports your brand, reputation, and expertise.

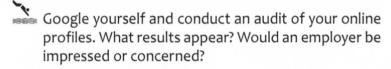 Google yourself and conduct an audit of your online profiles. What results appear? Would an employer be impressed or concerned?

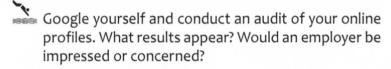 What do you want to be known for? How can you position yourself as an expert in your field?

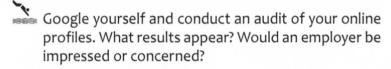 Are you sharing relative content on your field of expertise? Do your social profiles align with your career goals?

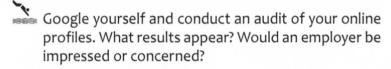 Are you following the Seven Cs to build your brand?

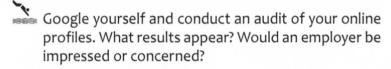 How are you adding value to your employer?

BUILD ENDURANCE

"Endurance is one of the most difficult disciplines, but it is to the one who endures that the final victory comes."
– Gautama Buddha

After 24 miles, my energy was fading. But my goal was in sight as I entered Central Park. Spurred on by the cheering crowds, I picked up my pace. I had worked hard over the last six months. I'd trained, planned, tracked, and logged every mile in pursuit of running the NYC Marathon.

As I ran through Central Park, I was overwhelmed with the prospect of achieving a major life goal of mine. At the 24-mile marker, I also saw my family. My dad says I hardly stopped to talk to them at that point. They were all jumping up and down, screaming, "You're almost there!" and, "You got this!" I hugged them quickly, then kept running. I was too close to the end. I needed to cross that finish line.

About 20 minutes later, I finished running the 2016 New York City Marathon.

For many years, life kept getting in the way of training for a marathon. But deep down inside, I never gave up on this goal. I repeatedly had put my dream of running the NYC Marathon on the backburner, even after starting to train. In fact, I had been training to run the NYC Marathon 15 years prior. I began logging my long runs and making great progress in 2001. At that time, I was not aware I was expecting a baby. Sadly, I experienced a miscarriage around September 15, 2001. Till this day, I believe the stress and horror of September 11 caused my miscarriage. Obviously, there is no way to know what exactly caused me to lose the baby. Though I was grateful to have my father alive following 9/11, the whole ordeal was extremely emotional and traumatic. Instead of getting depressed or frustrated, I stayed patient. I hoped that one year I would have a baby, and one year I would also run the NYC Marathon. Both happened.

When I completed the NYC Marathon in 2016, I ran it in honor of my Uncle Glenn Travers and all the lives lost on 9/11, including the baby I lost. I had my dream, my plan, and I also had purpose. I knew I needed to check this goal off my bucket list, and it was the right time to do it.

This is why the D.E.E.P. process is so important. Sometimes events or situations can get in the way of our desires, but we can get ourselves back on track with the right plan and timing. You can achieve your dreams, goals, and the life you desire and deserve if you create a plan and put in the required work to make it happen. It will require sacrifices, effort, and commitment, but you can make it happen. Yes, you will have obstacles and hurdles you can't control, but you can get past them with the right attitude. You can overcome adversity and hardship. The **Design** phase is all about leveraging your foundations, skills, and harnessing your dreams and desires to design your plans. The **Experience** phase requires you gaining the on-the-job knowledge and experience to get you on track and propel you forward. At that point, you can move into the **Execution** phase of the D.E.E.P. process. You owe it to yourself to execute on your dreams, plans, and goals. You deserve to take off and fly high. Don't do all the work that is required and not make the effort to execute on those plans. It means staying accountable, no excuses, and of course, a lot of hard work, but it will be worth it! Build the endurance in this phase to make it happen. The **Persevere** phase sets you up to soar and continue the path to achieve your dreams. Don't give up on your goals, desires, plans, and most of all, on yourself.

Throughout those years when I had to keep putting my dream on hold, I learned an important lesson about timing: To achieve any large and/or complicated goal, a plan is critical. Even when life throws you a curveball, you can always get back on track with your plans. You may need to reevaluate and adjust your timing, but don't give up. You can do almost anything you want when you're armed with determination and commitment. If you truly are dedicated to something, and you're capable of achieving it, you must make the commitment and put in the hard work to reach that goal. You need a plan of how to achieve your goal. What are you going to do along the way to make sure you get there?

Running a marathon and changing careers aren't all that different (as I've learned from working with numerous clients). For example, I once worked with a client named Julie who had left an academic job to seek a more lucrative and secure corporate job. Her background was in teaching and computer networking. Switching industries like this can take time, so while she looked for opportunities, I encouraged her to study the programming languages that employers were seeking to beef up her credentials. She mastered Python and created some sample programs to showcase her programming skills. Within four months, she landed a job with a national food service firm. What set Julie apart was that she systematically taught herself Python using free online tutorials and then went on to demonstrate her skills to potential employers. Learning Python wasn't a huge leap for her because she already knew several other programming languages. Consider how you can apply systematic determination to setting and reaching your career goals.

Enjoy the Journey

Training and running a marathon taught me many life lessons that stretch far beyond just running. These lessons were about living life, setting goals, finding balance, having resources and support, putting in the hard work and effort, and enjoying the experience.

Seriously, you've got to enjoy the experience. And I don't just mean the final race or goal—I mean the journey leading up to that goal. A great example I can share is that I missed the training after I was done running the marathon. Yes, believe it or not, I missed planning my runs, running my long routes on the weekend, and logging and tracking my progress.

I truthfully enjoyed the experience of planning to run the NYC Marathon *and* the run itself. That matters. I could have pushed myself through the experience. But that would not have been nearly as fun. And fun in and of itself is important.

This is another reason why self-knowledge is so important. I knew myself well enough to figure out how to transform what could be a difficult training and running experience into something that I would enjoy. That made my goal easier to sustain. I was happier—I was doing something that I wanted to do, which made fitting the training schedule into my life seamless. My family and colleagues were amiable to the occasional schedule disruption because I was confident and happy about what I was doing.

Career goals are much easier to achieve when they are enjoyable. Julie succeeded in her goal of mastering Python because she loved learning new coding languages. As a former English professor, she understood language and viewed coding as a fun skill to learn and one that would also advance her career. Because she was in between jobs, she didn't have a lot of spare cash to invest in acquiring new skills, so she creatively identified free online training resources. Then she figured out what she needed to learn, and she set up a schedule to accomplish her goals. She blocked off two hours every weekday afternoon for three months to learn the basics, then spent additional time working on projects to show potential employers.

Overcoming Obstacles

Although many people have achieved their dreams and goals, not everyone has overcome obstacles like those experienced by Amanda Gorman, the 23-year-old African American inaugural poet who recited her poem, *The Hill We Climb*, at President Joseph R. Biden's inauguration.[30] The daughter of a single mother born in Los Angeles, Gorman overcame an auditory processing disorder and speech articulation issues caused by her premature birth and chronic ear infections she experienced as a baby.[31]

These issues led to a speech impediment that required countless hours of practice to overcome. Her willingness to practice until she had mastery over her subject matter came in handy when preparing for the inauguration, as she did not want to stumble over her own words during her recitation. "For me, that takes a lot of energy and work," Gorman told The New York Times. "The writing process is its own excruciating form, but as someone with a speech impediment, speaking in front of millions of people presents its own type of terror."[32]

Gorman, who is the youngest inaugural poet in U.S. History, is a graduate of Harvard University.[33] Named as the first ever National Youth Poet Laureate in 2017, she was also commissioned to write a poem that was read at the 2021 Super Bowl.[34]

Then there's Kris Carr, who at age 32 was diagnosed with a rare and incurable Stage IV cancer on Valentine's Day, 2003.[35] Motivated to transform her life and live as long as possible, Carr wrote a series of best-selling self-help books and documentaries and launched a wellness brand and website.[36]

"I've been living with cancer for over a decade, and it has taught me so much about taking care of myself and living my life to the fullest," she said. "Although I still have cancer, I am healthy, and I run a mission-driven business that serves my community and makes me profoundly grateful every day. If I can pull that off, just imagine what YOU can do." [37]

When you think about what Amanda Gorman and Kris Carr have accomplished, you can understand the importance of dreaming big and not letting yourself get defeated by obstacles in the way of fulfilling those dreams. Dreaming big is a crucial state of mind that removes the boundaries and limitations we place on our capabilities.

Endurance Takeaways

Why do successful people emphasize goal setting to such a degree? Is it necessary to set goals if you want to achieve your dreams?

Yes, it is. Creating a systematic plan to achieve your goal helps you determine and reflect on what you have accomplished and how far you still must go to reach your dreams. Without a systematic plan, your efforts to achieve your dreams can become confusing and disjointed.

Often, a dream or goal may seem too time-consuming or too overwhelming. Breaking down the larger goal into smaller, attainable steps is of paramount importance.

When you go through this process, write down the required efforts and steps needed to reach your end objective. Most importantly, set specific deadlines for completing each step, thus creating a timeline to push you forward towards your dream. In the absence of specific deadlines, it is all too easy to postpone action steps and ultimately defer the achievement of your dream or objective.

As you navigate this process, you'll begin to see aspects of your goal that may not work. Maybe your original dream was not realistic. You may uncover potential barriers along the way, but don't let these obstacles stop you. Just modify your goals based on the new information you've unearthed, rethink your plan, and make any necessary adjustments. You'll be less discouraged by delays or detours that will inevitably happen. Perhaps your new plan and goals will be even better than your original ones.

In the end, the process of systematic planning, goal setting, and deadlines helps you focus and sustain the momentum required to achieve success. You cannot manage or improve what you cannot measure, and goal setting enables you to see what you may be lacking and where you need to progress.

Before you start setting goals for the different aspects of your life, you need to sit and think about what you truly desire from life. Reflecting on your priorities will help you determine what is most meaningful to you and how to prioritize your goals regarding these different aspects. This type of introspection is not something that you can accomplish in just a few minutes. Understand that your inner capabilities and desires require time and concentration. When you take time to figure out who you are and what you want, you will clarify your values. This type of in-depth personal analysis will clarify different aspects of your personality and align them with your goals and the person you want to be.

Every journey starts with a single step. By understanding who you are and who you want to be, you can take the necessary steps to set your goals and start your dream journey.

As Colin Powell said, "A dream does not become reality through magic; it takes sweat, determination, and hard work."

CHAPTER ELEVEN REFLECTION

We all require endurance in some capacity. It's not just about building up physical endurance. It's also about creating the mental toughness, grit, and confidence to overcome adversity and keep going to create the life you want. You also need to practice gratitude to keep a positive attitude. The older I get, the more I realize the importance of this practice. Often, a dream or goal may seem too time-consuming or too overwhelming—this is when you need endurance. Break down larger goals into smaller, attainable steps. This will help you keep moving forward. In the end, the process of systematic planning, goal setting, and deadlines helps you focus and sustain the momentum required to achieve success.

Think of a time where you had to build endurance. How did you push through challenges and obstacles?

How will you build endurance to accomplish your goals? What is your specific plan to achieve them?

Are you staying committed to your goals and following/tracking/logging your progress along the way?

Are you taking care of yourself mentally, physically, and spiritually?

Are you having fun along the way? Are you living in the moment? Are you choosing joy and gratitude?

STRATEGY 4

PERSEVERE:
MAKE A RIP ENTRY

BELIEVE IN YOURSELF

*"I love to see a young girl go out and grab
the world by the lapels. Life's a bitch.
You've got to go out and kick ass."*
– Maya Angelou

In my early 20s, I worked as an internal recruiter for a physician recruiting firm in Dallas. I was responsible for sourcing and screening candidates to be physician recruiters or sales representatives. The recruiters were then responsible for sourcing and screening doctors to work in smaller rural areas of the US. They worked long hours and spent many late nights and weekends calling their prospective doctor candidates.

The company monitored phone time and activity very closely. The sales representatives sold to hospitals and clinics in the rural areas. They were calling hospital administrators and doctors who led large practices. Their goal was to sell retained search services to the hospitals and clinics. When I joined the company, they were privately held and employed less than 100 people. The HR director (a woman) shared the profile of who we were looking to hire, described as the following:

- College degree, GPA 3.2 or better
- College athlete – played competitive sports, team-oriented
- Must be driven, ambitious, tenacious, and money motivated
- Strong communication skills, outgoing

- Professional image
- Willing to work late and on weekends

The positions offered a good base salary and bonus potential. Successful recruiters and sales reps were making six-figure incomes.

As I presented candidates to the directors and VPs, I quickly realized they were only interested in male candidates. I started to make it my mission to bring more female candidates into the company, but the leadership team seemed closed-minded. I talked with some of the directors about it, and their response was, "Joanie, the hospitals and clinics are good old boy networks. We need men to sell to them."

At this point in my career, I thought to myself, *I'm going nowhere fast here.* Even though I would have loved to step into a sales position with the company and prove them wrong, after two years, I chose to not fight the battle. I realized working for a male-dominated company that didn't believe women could be successful was not the environment I wanted to be a part of. Though I was competent, I didn't trust my employer to give me a chance to advance.

I knew I had value to offer, and I was ambitious to grow my career. But first, I needed to find a place that would allow me to spread my wings and fly. Luckily, a former colleague and good friend of mine, Shelley, had taken a new role expanding a professional staffing company in the southeast. She was looking to hire leaders to open new markets. I met with her and the leaders at the company, and they sold me on the chance to be a manager and open a brand-new office in Atlanta, Georgia. I would be responsible for hiring a team and growing the business from scratch. I was thrilled to join a company that so clearly believed in me.

At the same time, I wanted to march into the CEO's office at the physician recruiting firm and tell him I was resigning because they weren't hiring or promoting women at his firm. I wanted to tell him he would regret never putting me in sales or leadership, and that he'd made a huge mistake not offering me more opportunity.

But I didn't.

I held my head high and resigned with grace. You see, I was taught not to burn bridges. You never know when paths may cross again, and this industry can be small. I was also in a very junior role, just starting out in my career. I didn't want to cause any waves. So, I kept the message simple and gave my two-weeks' notice.

I packed up my apartment in Dallas into a U-Haul and drove to Atlanta with my good friend, Jim. I knew I was taking a risk, but I believed in myself. I had goals and plans for advancing my career, and I had the confidence in myself to take the chance. Had I chosen to stay in a company that didn't value me and my contributions, I'm certain I would've been miserable. I needed to make the change, pursue my ambitions, and invest in my career growth.

Taking the new position in Atlanta was one of the riskiest and best moves I ever made. It was the springboard that catapulted me into leadership in the staffing industry. I was able to take the next step in my career, and I was on track to achieve new goals and aspirations. Over the next few years, I hired an amazing team of people, and we accomplished many special milestones together. We built an office from nothing into a multi-million-dollar location, and it became one of the fastest growing and most profitable offices in the company's history. We gained recognition and awards, and we benefited financially from our hard work and success.

Years later, I was promoted to a vice president role. There, I expanded my territory and took on more responsibility. Ironically, the company I was working for had operations in the same building as the physician recruiting firm in Dallas. One day while I was visiting Dallas, I decided to go visit my old employer. Wearing one of my best suits, I rode up the elevator, walked into the lobby, and strutted over to the CEO's office. I explained I was in the building and just wanted to stop by and say hello. He was happy to see me and asked what I was up to. I proudly told him about my current role and shared my success over the last few years. He looked pleased, but I could sense he was also curious about why I'd stopped by.

After a few minutes, I decided to get to the point. I looked him right in his eyes and said, "The real reason I stopped by is to let you know that you made a mistake not putting me into a sales role years ago. I would have been a great asset for you and the company. No hard feelings, though. That decision propelled me to follow my dreams. Now I'm in a great position that I love. I want to thank you for the experience I had working here, and for the lessons I learned. They were valuable. I wish you and your firm the best."

He looked at me, surprised. Then, humbly, he said, "You're right, Joanie. I should have put you in sales. If you ever want to come back, please reach out."

Whether he meant it or not didn't matter. I was glad I spoke up.

I thanked him for his time and left. I rode down that elevator proud of myself for getting closure. Proud of myself for speaking up. Most of all, I was proud of myself and grateful for leaving that company years prior. I'd put my career aspirations first, and I'd won.

Years passed, in which I continued to climb the ladder at my current employer. I advanced my career and assumed additional responsibility. By then I was in my late 20s, in a position where I was being promoted to a role that required me to start managing my peers. I remember approaching a colleague who would now be one of my direct reports. Doug was a gentleman in his mid-50s, an experienced and successful executive recruiter and manager. Doug and I had always maintained a strong working relationship filled with mutual respect. We got along very well. But now I was his boss. I wondered how he felt about the prospect of reporting to me. Did he feel he deserved the role I'd been given? Let's face the stereotypes for a minute here: He was a white male in his 50s, and I was a female in my late 20s. I figured he would be uncomfortable.

However, I'd learned to never underestimate the value of relationships. In every interaction you have with a coworker, you demonstrate three important values: trust, competency, and care. My incredibly insightful executive coach, Mike, had told me that people will work for someone if they know their boss possesses these three main traits. This trifecta is powerful, often propelling your relationships and career to the next level.

1. **Trust:** "Is my boss trustworthy?" is one of the first questions you'll likely consider when you get a new boss. You want to know if your supervisor has your back and is willing to work for your best interests. Without trust, it's impossible to forge a positive, collaborative working relationship.
2. **Competence:** "Is my boss competent?" is another question you'll consider with any new boss. Working for someone who lacks the skills to do their job is painful and difficult.
3. **Care:** "Does my boss care about me?" is probably the most important question of the three. You

want to work for someone who exhibits care and concern for those they supervise. Bosses who lack that quality can leave you feeling disconnected and alienated from your employer. And at that point, you may start wondering if it's time to look for a new job.

With these principles in mind, I decided to meet with Doug face-to-face. I wanted to address the elephant in the room right from the start. Mike had told me that people may be able to live with two out of three things for a while— but if they can't answer yes to at least two of those three critical questions, they won't feel committed to the boss, the organization, or their role.

Although I'd truly earned my promotion, I wanted to establish a bond with Doug and the other employees I would be supervising. I wanted to reassure my team that I was trustworthy, competent, and caring. As we talked, I relaxed. I quickly realized that the equation of trust, competency, and caring had laid the foundation for the next phase of our work relationship. Doug already knew I was caring. He knew I was competent, and he trusted me. And I felt the same about him.

I'm proud to say we recognized we were stronger together. We built plans, set goals, and achieved success—together. I will always cherish the experience and relationship I had with Doug. I am grateful for his open mind and acceptance of me. I am grateful that we both gave each other a chance.

As time passed, our working and personal relationship further blossomed. We were true partners and colleagues, and I cherish the time we worked together. Over the years, I learned about his family, his kids, his grandkids, and eventually his battle with cancer. I am sad to say that a few years ago, Doug passed away. I was heartbroken to lose him as a friend and colleague. But at the same time, I was eternally grateful for all the lessons he taught me—both directly and indirectly. He helped me be a better leader. He helped me see that it isn't about age, race, or color. It's all about the way you treat one another and relate to each other.

Just Say "No"

An interesting side note about the position I had been promoted to was that I succeeded someone who'd only had the position for a short period of time. Previously, I was informed that a counterpart I'd worked alongside for several years, Victor, was being promoted to senior vice president and would be my new boss. While he was always the life of the party and had a successful track record, I was shocked to see him get this big promotion. I remember shaking my head and thinking, *this is part of the "good old boys' network," which I might have to accept.* But deep down, I was not happy about reporting to him.

Looking back on Victor's career, I believe he did a much better job of promoting himself than he did delivering strong results. Not long after he started this job, we were at a conference together.

Noticing me, Victor came over, reached out his hand, and said, "Joanie. I'm looking forward to working with you. I know you've done a great job in your territory and that you'll continue to produce results."

"Thanks," I replied, shaking his hand. "Congratulations on the promotion!"

But a few months later, our cordial dynamic changed. During happy hour at a national conference, he approached me at the bar and made a pass at me.

"Joanie," he said confidently, leaning towards me, "I'm just saying—I'm willing if you are."

I flinched, thinking, *really? Not what I need to deal with from my new boss.*

At that moment, I didn't care if he fired me. While he might have been competent, he clearly didn't care about me, and he *was not* trustworthy. I could only check off one out of three traits my executive coach talked about. I didn't want to work for someone I didn't trust and who didn't care. I didn't want to work for someone with no morals or ethics. Instead of following my gut instinct, which was to resign on the spot, I looked him right in the eye and said, "I am not willing." Then I walked away.

It was one of the most empowering and scary moments of my career. I figured he would let me go the following week, but I didn't care. I would not stoop to that level, nor did I need to. I figured if he didn't fire me, I would search for a new role and eventually resign. Strangely enough, neither happened. You see, Victor was on a path of self-destruction. He didn't end up being my boss for very long. It doesn't always work out that way, but in this case it did. Shortly after that incident, he was fired for other reasons. Did I mention I believe in karma? Well, I do.

To have integrity is to live life according to your morals, principles, and values. To have integrity, you must have a clear sense of what you consider to be right and wrong, and of your perspective on the main purpose in your life. Believing in yourself and staying committed to your goals and aspirations needs to be your priority. I encourage you to persevere and protect yourself through the challenges and obstacles that life throws you. You will be better and stronger for it.

The CEO soon realized he'd made a big mistake promoting Victor, who was quickly removed without me having to say anything. In retrospect, I should have spoken up. This was over 20 years ago, long before the #MeToo movement. Regardless, I have no regrets about what transpired. I am thankful for the confidence and support I've received from my parents, family, and friends to know that I needed to stand up for myself. I'm grateful for the gift of confidence in myself and the confidence to say "no." To say "hell no."

CHAPTER TWELVE REFLECTION

It's important to maintain integrity in your career and in life—but it's equally important to work in a mutually respectful environment. Believe in yourself and stay confident in your values. Don't let anyone tell you that you can't do something. If trust, honesty, or integrity is missing in key work relationships, a change may be in order. Know your worth and never compromise your values.

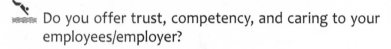 Do you offer trust, competency, and caring to your employees/employer?

 Does your employer offer them to you?

Do you know where you draw the line when it comes to compromising your morals or values at work? Are there any areas you need to adjust or refocus?

Review your values and goals to ensure you are on track with your priorities.

GRACE & GRIT

"Courage is grace under pressure."
– Ernest Hemingway

As I mentioned in previous chapters, early in my career, I was in a position where I was leading managers who were about twice my age. While others might have been intimidated, I jumped at the chance, eager to advance my career as quickly as possible. I was young—naïve and confident at the same time—and really didn't know what I was signing up for, which was perhaps just as well.

Fortunately, for the managers I supervised, the company invested in building my skills by hiring an executive coach to work with me. I mentioned my executive coach, Mike, and some of his fabulous advice in Chapter 12, "Believe in Yourself." I have no doubt having an executive coach accelerated my success as I continued to rise through the organization. I wouldn't be where I am today if it weren't for Mike and my boss, Tom, who both invested in me. I'm so grateful for the wisdom, guidance, and honest feedback I gained from them.

Having a coach is a gift—one I am eternally grateful for. Mike's guidance, insights, and ability to help me understand how to use my strengths and compensate for my weaknesses were a game changer. Competitive divers (or any athlete, for that matter) benefit from an athletic coach who can improve technique, overall performance, and increase their success. Career or executive coaches can help you achieve greater results and achievements at work.

The key is that you must be open to the coaching, advice, and owning how you can improve. Some people might be intimidated by a coach, but their job is to help you perform better. If you get the chance to have an executive coach, I recommend you embrace them and make the most of the opportunity. Leverage this person to help you achieve greater results in all you do. That's their job.

About a year after my promotion to an SVP role, Mike and I happened to be at the same conference in Dallas. We had a chance to grab a drink after the last session. I ordered my usual glass of chardonnay, and he ordered his favorite scotch. It was nice to have a moment to just sit, relax, and catch up in a casual setting.

At one point in our conversation, he said: "Joanie, I would describe you as a boxer with velvet gloves."

"What do you mean?" I said, looking at him inquisitively.

"Your graceful and thoughtful approach in dealing with others is like knocking someone out" he said. "People get the message, but you do it in a way where they don't feel beaten down. You know how to deliver a tough message, hit them directly, but they can still walk away a better person. Don't lose this trait. Not many people have the necessary grace and grit to do that. These characteristics are your secret weapons. They will take you far."

Recognizing a major compliment, I smiled. But I was also a bit stunned. I'd never thought of myself the way he described: as someone who delivers a punch, but with a soft touch.

Later, after having a chance to think through what he'd said, the words resonated with me. Somehow, somewhere, I had gained the ability to deliver constructive criticism or a difficult message in a kind, thoughtful way. Perhaps it was my upbringing—I was raised to be a compassionate person. Whatever it was, I was happy to realize that my core values of kindness and consideration not only translated to the business world, but they were making me be a better leader.

In time, I began to truly understand how the equation of kindness, grace, and brutal honesty translates into powerful, meaningful leadership. Conventional wisdom dictates that women who are "too nice" or "too feminine" may not be leadership material, especially when women have historically struggled for equality and recognition in the workplace and in many cultures around the world. On the other hand, women who are perceived as mean, "bitchy," or difficult to work with may not be trusted by their peers or subordinates. While they will likely be viewed as driven, they also may struggle to connect with others in building long-lasting professional partnerships.

Unfortunately, many believe that kind, polite women are unsuited for challenging leadership roles. I find this attitude baffling—since when does kindness disqualify you from making difficult decisions or holding challenging conversations? Perhaps they assume that if you're a kind, considerate person, you will be unable to hold others accountable. I understood that what my coach counted as an asset has been viewed by others as a liability. They thought I didn't have the ability to make the necessary tough calls. Meanwhile, if you looked at my track record of success in growing sales and profits, you wouldn't question my ability for a second. If my financial performance was laid out in front of you, it would show a story of continued success and an ability to drive outstanding results through economic downturns and even a global pandemic.

Leaders who truly care about the long-term growth of their team and the organization are not nice. Instead, they are kind. Kindness shows you care about the person. You care about their well-being and success. And as I've said, working for someone who cares about you is critical to a collaborative, supportive working relationship. Kindness has been a secret weapon for me. It doesn't make me soft, but it gives me that soft touch like the boxer with velvet gloves. People know I care, and my intentions are to drive better results and improved performance.

For example, simply being nice when giving feedback just means saying positive things. Whereas being kind when giving feedback requires helping another person understand how to improve. It means sometimes having to tell people things they don't want to hear.

Think of an accomplished diver. They possess both grace and grit. They need mental toughness, physical strength, and the grace to move quickly but smoothly. They perform their dive by beautifully entering the water with hardly a splash. It is called a rip entry. A rip entry is one of the most valuable and difficult skills to master in diving and takes years of practice to perfect. I use this analogy to point out how mental toughness and grace can make a powerful combination. I believe the same combination can be a secret weapon in business—a very powerful weapon. You need mental toughness. You need to be skilled. You need to move quickly on the right decisions. And most of all, if you do it gracefully and with kindness, you will achieve amazing results.

Hannah Krimm was Georgia Tech's first female diving All-American athlete and she describes her sport as the following. "Diving has taught me a lot about life. My sport is all about perseverance and hard work. Sometimes you fail and sometimes you have to overcome obstacles and you learn you have to stay calm. It seems like those are the same things you need in your daily life." Grit provides the perseverance and work ethic to overcome obstacles, while grace provides the calmness to get you through the difficult times.

Kindness and consideration don't automatically cancel out competency and effectiveness. So why do people question someone who is kind and thoughtful when it comes to driving results and making difficult decisions? It's a great question, one that may be impossible for me—on the other side of the equation—to answer. But I know from my own experience and decades of working with other kind and considerate individuals that you don't have to be "hard" to move up in this world. I have seen and worked with many people who have a sharp edge to their style. These people can be successful, but their style isn't the only path to success. In fact, I've also seen sharp-edged leaders struggle to hang on to talent—many are turned off by a brusque manner.

Regardless of your core values and personality traits, to get ahead you must be mentally tough, determined, and hard working. As I mentioned earlier, there are similarities in what it takes to succeed in business and what it takes to run a marathon. From my experience, the ability to complete a marathon has a lot more to do with your mental toughness than your physical ability. Staying focused on your goals, believing in yourself, and persisting regardless of the conditions—*those* are the keys to success.

During many points in my career, I would present to the CEO or board of directors of a publicly traded company and at the end of the meeting, I would look around and realize: *I'm one the only woman in the room.* I remember one such incident at a meeting filled with about 40 New York investment bankers and business leaders, with one other female colleague sitting at one end of the table. After observing the population of the room, I leaned over to my colleague and commented: "Look at all these men and the lack of diversity in the room."

Not only was it a room filled with men—they were all *white* men. This sad situation made me stop and think. I asked myself, when will we start to see more of a balance in the workplace at the higher levels of the organization? Will it be in my lifetime? Will my daughter or grandchildren see a more diverse workplace?

On a particularly long day of executive board meetings, one moment stood out for me to ignite more female representation at the board level: a member of the company's all-male board of directors announced his retirement. After dinner, a few of us sat around the table, batting around ideas for future strategies. As we were wrapping up, the chairman and a few of the current board members came over to the table. The chairman was very complimentary regarding our outstanding performance and presentations. Laughter echoed throughout the room amid friendly conversations. It was one of the better board meetings I'd attended.

The conversation turned to the opening on the board. Prospective candidates were being floated. *This is the moment*, I thought.

Turning to the chairman and the other nearby board members, I said in a non-abrasive and upbeat tone: "I think it's time we find a female candidate for the open seat. It would be great if we had some diversity on our board of directors. I believe it would bring a fresh perspective."

Did you really want to say that out loud? My inner voice protested. But the words had left my lips—it was too late.

Maybe the red wine at dinner softened my filter. While my suggestion was polite, it was also firm. This was a grace with grit moment. In all honesty, I'd been wanting to confront the chairman and the board about having more diversity at the top for some time. I had a hard time working for an employment agency that failed to represent equal opportunity at the top.

As I looked around the room, I could see one of my colleagues looking at me with a warning sign that said: You may have just put your foot in your mouth or committed a career-limiting move.

There was a minute of awkward silence. I smiled and looked over at the chairman, waiting for him to acknowledge my comment.

"You are right, Joanie," he said. "We could use a little diversity. It's something we have discussed and are focused on."

"I'm glad to hear that" I said. "I know many women at our company would like to see more diversity on the board."

Another board member chimed in, "Joanie, we can't have a woman on the board. If we had a female board member, she would make us work in our meetings and hold us accountable for getting things done."

Everyone burst out in laughter. I laughed and smiled too— but I also thought to myself, *there is probably some truth to that statement.*

Board Diversity

Although diversity has improved on corporate boards, more progress is necessary. As of the second quarter of 2022, only 28% of corporate board seats at North American companies were held by women.[38] Although this is an increase from the 25.6% of seats held by women in 2021, the pace was slower than the 3% rise seen the previous year.[39] When looking at Fortune 500 companies, just 31% of board members are female, and that number drops to a staggering 7% for non-white women.[40]

Clearly, women and other underrepresented populations have a long way to go to achieve equity on the boards of publicly traded companies. The point I want to make is that there should be more focus on the benefits of equity, diversity, and inclusion rather than just the idea of equity for the sake of equity. I believe a focus on the advantages of this approach will help more than generalized advocacy.

Catalyst, citing a 2006 study from the Wellesley Centers for Women, reports that, "Research shows when women hold at least three seats, this 'critical mass' is good for corporate governance."[41] The Yale School of Management noted that "Research shows having a critical mass of women on a board leads to higher quality decision making, reduced operational risk, faster innovation and better financial results on many key metrics."[42]

An article entitled "Gender Diversity at the Board Level Can Mean Innovation Success," published in the MIT Sloan Management Review, stated, "Studies suggest that gender diversity can play an important role in supporting innovative activity and organizational change. For example, companies with greater gender diversity are associated with higher R&D intensity, obtain more patents, and report higher levels of overall innovation (particularly when there is a critical mass of women directors). This pattern is also reflected in external accolades; companies recognized as innovators have more women directors."[43]

These statistics and research reflect my experience seeing women struggle for equality in the workplace and in cultures around the world. Although there have been some advancements in recent years due to the emphasis on diversity, equity, and inclusion, progress is still too slow. Frankly, reading the reports makes me disheartened and frustrated. I want to see more women on executive boards and more diversity at the top levels of all organizations.

Success Comes in Many Flavors

I have always been bossy. In fact, I'm known as "the boss" in my family. Growing up, I was the oldest of four girls, so I naturally took charge of things. My parents joke that I was in charge as soon as I started talking. But why is being bossy looked at as a negative quality for women but as an asset for men?

I love that Sheryl Sandberg, former COO of Facebook, addressed this sentiment in her book, *Lean In*. She wrote, "In my 25 years, I have worked with and experienced many different styles of leadership from females and males. There is no one perfect leader or style but I have observed the most successful leaders do possess a combination of grace and grit. They use their persuasion skills to influence others in the direction they want to go, and they aren't afraid to roll up their sleeves and show you they can and will get the job done. They lead by example, and they set the tone for the organization. They care about the business, the people and the results and they will make the difficult decisions to execute the strategy and plans to get the job done. It doesn't matter if they are male or female. What matters is how they handle themselves in leading and executing the strategy to move things forward in the right direction."[44]

Having grace and grit can also help you have tough conversations with employees, leaders, customers, friends, and family. I have always liked the saying, "You catch more bees with honey," but I am also the type of person who wants to get to the point. I believe the secret to having productive and difficult conversations is clearly communicating the message in a respectful tone and manner. Our world would be a better place if we had more grit with grace.

I'm also happy to report that the next appointee to the board of directors was a female with a strong track record of success and a diverse range of experience and accomplishments. She brought grace and grit to the board and was a welcome addition.

CHAPTER THIRTEEN REFLECTION

Practice the difference between being kind vs. nice both at work and in personal relationships or situations. Being nice works well with strangers, but leaders who care about the long-term growth of their teams are not nice. They can be kind, though. Regardless of the motive, leaders who practice nice leadership do whatever it takes to keep the peace. However, while avoidance of awkward situations or difficult conversations may work in the short-term, allowing problems to fester hurts morale and ultimately negatively impacts everyone—including the underperforming individual. Difficult conversations don't have to be delivered in a cold or scathing manner; instead, find ways to embrace the grace and grit philosophy. Know your secret weapons and stay true to who you are at your core.

 What are your secret weapons? How can you best use them to propel you further?

 Are you being direct, clear, and respectful when having difficult or challenging conversations?

 Can you think of a time when you responded with niceness (i.e., superficial words or simple gestures) when you and the other person would have been better served by kindness (i.e., expressed through actions or helping people?

 Can you think of a time when you thought someone was being mean or unfair to you, but they may have in fact been acting kind?

TAKE A TIMEOUT

"Sometimes you need to unplug to recharge. We are human, not a Tesla."
– Michael D. Bixler

As you learned from my previous chapters, I find much enjoyment in running. Running is one of my outlets to think and clear my mind. It gives me time to myself and is a great stress reducer. After a run and especially a long run, I also enjoy the ability to rest, stretch, rehydrate, and recover. The recovery is a process, and if you do it appropriately, you become stronger, faster, run longer, and ultimately become a better runner.

When I reached my late 40s, I realized I was running pretty hard in life and not taking the time to renew myself and recharge my batteries. I needed to spend a bit more time focusing on my mind and my soul. I was working around the clock, traveling every week, and coping with a challenging personal situation at home. I knew I needed to create a healthier lifestyle for myself and my family.

I was facing the decision of getting divorced, again. It was a devastating period in my life and a complicated situation because I didn't want to get divorced or be divorced. However, I realized my family was struggling, and our home was not filled with joy. Everyone was walking around on eggshells, and we couldn't live like that anymore. More importantly, it was affecting my children's well-being.

I decided I had to make some changes in my life, and I had to prioritize myself and my kids, who were young teenagers at the time. I decided to rent a home that would be a safe place for all of us to have space while I tried to work things out and make some decisions.

This was the start of a new personal journey—one that saw me spending more time alone and prioritizing self-care. I changed the way I spent my days. My morning rituals became sacred time for me to read, pray, write, and meditate. I had always heard that time alone in meditation can change your life and be so good for your soul, but it wasn't until I started to practice this daily that I started to see a true change in my attitude and in my mind. It helped me see things clearly. It gave me time and space to work through some difficult decisions. I went to bed earlier, got a restful night's sleep, and I rose early every day. I cherished my quiet mornings, and I knew my mind and soul were flourishing in this peaceful and quiet time.

I spent the next year working on myself and my relationship with my kids. I had some repairs to do in both regards. I was beating myself up for not making changes sooner. I worked with a therapist and found a good therapist for my kids as well. To say it was a difficult or challenging time would be an understatement, but it was a period of personal growth. Over time, my relationship with my kids strengthened. I also became stronger and saw things clearly. I was able to focus on myself. I realized I was okay being alone. I didn't need another human to make me happy—because happiness lives inside of me. In fact, I enjoyed having time and the ability to focus on myself. I treasured my quiet space, and had more time to spend writing, reading, and meditating.

During this time, I kept reflecting on the bible scripture, *Galatians 5:22-23: "In contrast, the fruit of the Spirit is love, joy, peace, patience, kindness, generosity, faithfulness, gentleness, and self-control. There is no law against such things."*[23] This scripture kept me focused on finding joy in my life and gave me the permission to be gentle with myself.

We need to own our issues, happiness, and embrace opportunities to live our best lives. You can't do it for someone else. I couldn't be in a healthy relationship with someone else if I wasn't in a joyful and happy place with myself. I couldn't be the best mom, daughter, friend, girlfriend, employee, or boss unless I was in the best place I could be. I needed to make sure I had my priorities straight and that I was clear about what I really wanted in life. I needed to focus on what was most important to me and what was most important in the relationships that I had with others. Having time alone gave me insight into myself and clarity about what really mattered to me. Spending time alone to think, reflect and recharge, is a constructive self-improvement process that can change your life.

I encourage you to spend time daily giving thanks for all the blessings in your life. What makes you happy? What sparks joy in your life? As my daughter told her brother when she was five years old, "Focus on the good things and you'll have a happy life." Gratefulness can help you live in the moment. Make your attitude filled with gratitude. It's everything.

Timeout from Academics & Work

Sometimes students take a gap year before entering graduate school or furthering their education. A gap year, or a sabbatical, can offer a break from academic studies and an opportunity to pursue work, internships, travel, or maybe a volunteer opportunity. The same timeout principle of having space, time to think, and step away from the day-to-day grind can be priceless. Friends have asked me my thoughts on their children taking a gap year before they enter grad school and I always encourage it, with the stipulation that they must do something productive. A gap year before college or grad school is meant to be filled with learning new skills, and a chance to gain experience. It should help a student gain clarity on their future and where they want to focus.

One of my clients created a unique program offering their employees the opportunity to take a 6-month paid sabbatical. I thought it was a brilliant employee retention strategy, but it also provided so many other benefits. Once an employee had worked for the firm for 7 years, they were eligible to apply for the program. In their application, they had to outline how they would be spending their time and what they hoped to gain from the time off. In addition, they had to recommend someone who could cover their responsibilities while they were out. They used this as an opportunity for a stretch assignment for lower-level workers. It was a chance for others to learn new responsibilities and try new things. Once the sabbatical was over, the employee would come back and debrief on their time and what they gained from the experience. The leadership team shared that those employees always came back well rested, energized, and with a fresh perspective. Taking the time away always provided the refresh and recharge the employee needed. Once again, proving the importance of time to step away, see things clearly, and recharge those batteries.

Don't ever waste the gift of time. Don't take a gap year or sabbatical and lay around and do nothing. If you are taking time off, I encourage you to make the most of it. It will require some planning and goal setting, but it could be one of the most valuable and productive life experiences.

The Benefits of a Pandemic

Ironically, after spending a good amount of time by myself, I was forced into another year of isolation. As we all know, in March of 2020 the world shut down due to the coronavirus pandemic. I recognize this was one of the most challenging and devastating times for many families who lost loved ones. Obviously, it had rippling effects on our economy and our workforce. COVID-19 was a life-changing event, but I have to say it was a blessing for my children and me. It gave me a green light and an opportunity to slow down and spend more quality time in my home with my children. This gift of time was one that I will be eternally grateful for.

During this period, I learned some new things about myself. I learned I actually could cook, and that I enjoyed doing so. I've never considered myself a good cook, but I realized that was because I never gave it the time or effort. I was too busy with other priorities. And the truth is I just didn't care that much about cooking. Being home forced me to cook and changed the way I thought about it. I now looked forward to having dinner as a family every night. I wanted to make something special that we would all enjoy. I found myself taking time to research recipes and plan out different meals. I even took a few online cooking classes and learned how to make an amazing lasagna, pizza, and a few other new dishes. I learned it's never too late to learn something new. I needed to slow down and enjoy the cooking experience.

I also learned that I needed to stop and smell the roses. I spent time planting flowers and created a small vegetable garden. I had never had that much free time to myself, but I found myself doing things that I always wished I had time to do. Though I missed seeing family, friends, and coworkers, I realized I needed to have the time to myself. I realized I am a bit more of an introvert than I previously admitted.

I like my time alone. I get to think, create, and take care of myself. And most importantly, I don't feel guilty for spending time alone or doing the things that I want to do. (Oh, that Catholic guilt can do a number on you!)

Most of all, I realized my kids and my dog were my favorite people to hang out with. I was so grateful for our special time together. I will never forget the evening golf cart rides, watching the sunset together, bike rides, family dinners, playing games, family workouts, and charades in the swimming pool. These were joyful times, and it was an amazing gift to just be present in the moment and bond with my children. I felt rested, renewed, and had a full heart. I had unplugged and was completely recharged.

I believe the gift of time alone to reflect, to renew ourselves and grow spiritually, can help propel us forward. It can be the secret to moving up in life. I'm not talking about moving up the corporate ladder. Moving up is about moving yourself up to a better place in your mind, body, and spirit. It is about being comfortable in your own skin and having clarity about what you want and should do next. It is about making the right decisions and understanding the implications of those choices. It is about moving yourself forward to believe in yourself and have the confidence to pursue your dreams and live your best life. Moving up is about finding your true self and what it takes to experience joy.

As you've read in Chapter 4, "Dream Big," you know how passionate I am about goal setting, dreaming big, and overcoming adversity. I've spoken about the importance of believing in yourself and having confidence to step up and step into your best life. I've shared stories on gaining experience and leveraging knowledge to propel you forward. I've shared stories on the importance of mentors and stretch assignments to take you further. I've talked about the importance of building up endurance, putting in the work, being accountable, and making it happen. I believe all these things are vitally important to living your best life and achieving your desired career path. However, I want to emphasize this point in particular: I believe the most important thing you can do is take the time to work on yourself to make sure you are on the right track.

Don't try and fool yourself or waste precious time thinking things will get better. If you're not in the right career or the right relationship, or you're not on the right trajectory with how you want to live your life, I want to give you permission to take a time out. Give yourself the gift of some space to think. Give yourself the gift of time to evaluate what's most important to you. It will be life-changing. If you're in a situation where you feel like you can't step away, I would encourage you to wake up an hour earlier to have that quiet time to yourself in the morning, or prioritize having a quiet hour in the evening. Maybe you need to go for a long walk in the afternoon by yourself so you can just think. There are ways to find some down time for yourself and let yourself explore what's important to you. There are ways to make sure you're evaluating your priorities. Make sure you use this time wisely. Don't get on your phone or check emails from work. I refer to it as P.T.O.—not paid time off, but protected timeout. You need your daily P.T.O.!

Keep a journal. New ideas, thoughts, and memories will hit you during your daily P.T.O., and you'll want to write them down. You will have good days and bad, but it is important to capture your thoughts and ideas. Write down what is important to you. Keep referring back to your journal over time. It can be helpful when you are evaluating changes, decisions, or ideas that relate to creating the life you want to have.

You must believe you deserve the best life possible. Don't settle for anything else. It will take work. It will take effort.

You will need to commit to personal growth and improving the things or situations that aren't working in your life. It's more than okay to get support from family, friends, or professionals. But the responsibility to make it happen lies with you.

Though our journeys are different, we are all in it together. We can provide strength and support to one another. However, if you're looking for someone to carry you through this process or journey, you are probably in the wrong place. You can gain advice, support, love, and experience from coaches, friends, and family. But it's up to you to make the choices and own the process. Love yourself enough to know that you deserve your best life. Now go make it happen!

CHAPTER FOURTEEN REFLECTION

The most important thing you can do to live your best life and career is take the time to work on yourself to make sure you are on the right track. The gift of time alone to reflect, to renew ourselves, and to grow spiritually can help propel us forward and be the secret to moving up in life. Not just moving up in your career, but moving yourself up to a better place in your mind, body, and spirit. It is about being comfortable in your own skin and having clarity about what you want and what you should do next. Commit to believing in yourself. Embrace the confidence to pursue your dreams and live your best life.

 Are you making time for, and prioritizing, YOU?

 How can you set aside time for yourself to think, dream, and reflect daily? Take your P.T.O.

 What are you grateful for? Are you spending a few minutes every morning or evening listing three or four positive things you are grateful for?

 Are you keeping a journal and referring to it often enough?

SPEAK UP

"Do one thing every day that scares you."
– Eleanor Roosevelt

With a New Year approaching, I scheduled a meeting with my CEO, Tom, to discuss business goals and budgets. I had big plans for my division in the upcoming year and was excited to share them with him.

We met and discussed the strategic growth plan for the year. Tom was pleased, but I knew something was missing. I realized I needed to enlarge the scope of the conversation to articulate my personal career goals and aspirations.

"Tom, as you know, I love my current position. But I want you to know that down the road, I would like to take on a larger role," I said, smiling and putting down my cup of coffee. "My kids are both in high school, but once they both move on to college, I know I can take on and do more. I want to make sure I'm preparing myself for a larger position. Do you have any suggestions for me?"

Looking surprised, Tom replied, "Joanie, you have a ton of potential, and I am glad to hear you want to do more."

He paused and took a sip of his coffee. Then he continued, "You're doing a great job of running your division. You've successfully worn a bunch of different hats for our company. Let me give your question some thought, and I will get back to you."

As the silence between us lengthened, I realized my comment might have taken him by surprise. He wasn't expecting me to say I wanted a bigger role. Maybe I'd scared him off—was he thinking I might want to leave my current role or the company?

Moving to advance the conversation and quell any doubts, I quickly said, "Let me clarify that I am not looking to leave the company. I just want to make sure I am doing everything I can to position myself for larger roles and growth in the future."

As we wrapped up our meeting, Tom looked directly at me and said, "I'm glad you spoke up and told me your interests. Thank you."

Time passed. I kept busy running and growing my division. Travel filled my schedule as the business grew.

Then, one Friday afternoon, I arrived in Fort Lauderdale airport after a few days away. As the plane taxied to the gate, I checked my phone and started listening to my voice messages.

"I know you're traveling. But give me a call when you land," Tom said.

Oh no, I thought. *It's Friday afternoon and Tom wants to talk to me—it must be bad news!*

Calming myself down, I realized there was no way to know what he was going to say until I talked to him. First, I would retrieve my luggage and get my car. I wanted to be in a quiet place—where I could brace myself for whatever he was going to tell me late on a Friday.

Finally, I called him.

"Tom, I got your message. Is everything okay?"

"Yes!" he said jovially. "Thanks for getting back to me. I just wanted to give you a heads up on something. Since I'm nearing retirement, I've decided that I need to cut back on some responsibilities. One of those is my seat on the board of directors of the American Staffing Association."

Oh no, I thought. Tom is going to be retiring and leaving the company. This is not good.

Before I could venture into more speculation, Tom's voice jerked me back to reality.

"I'm not retiring tomorrow. But I was thinking about what you said about getting ready for a larger role in the future," he continued. "So, I had an idea. I would like to nominate you to take my seat on the American Staffing Association board. I believe this would be a great opportunity and exposure for you, and I think you would be great for the role."

I was flattered. Humbled. Pleasantly surprised.

"Tom, thank you," I said enthusiastically. "I would be thrilled to be nominated and especially honored to take your seat on the board. Thank you for thinking of me."

Shortly after I arrived home, while I was unpacking my suitcase, my cell phone rang.

"Joanie, this is Richard Wahlquist, the CEO of the American Staffing Association. I understand Tom has connected with you and mentioned the opportunity to join the ASA board. I wanted to talk to you about that."

During a wide-ranging conversation, Richard outlined the role of the American Staffing Association in the staffing industry and the responsibilities of the board. By the end of the call, I told Richard I would be honored to join the board.

After that call, I realized how grateful I was that I had spoken up to Tom regarding my desire for advancement. If I had not told him about my career ambitions and my desires to take on a larger role, the ASA opportunity may have never arisen for me. I had planted the seed in the mind of my boss that I wanted the opportunity to learn and prepare for a greater role in the future. And when the opportunity arose, he thought of me. If I hadn't spoken up, he might have referred someone else or given up his seat without nominating a replacement. The power of speaking up and sharing your personal goals and vision is so important.

Importance of Articulating Goals

Have you ever heard people say that you need to put your thoughts, desires, and dreams out into the universe and then see what happens? Well, I am living proof that it works!

You need to let your boss, colleagues, family, and network know about your goals and ambitions. You need to speak up. You need to share your desires and plans with others. When you share your dreams and desires with others, you get one step closer to bringing them to fruition. There is also something magical about verbalizing your goals and ambitions with others. When you share your ambitions with others, you are verbally committing your goals with others. You put it out there, so you need to follow through. You can't just say you want to do it. Tell others *what* you want to do and *how* you plan to get there. Let them help you get there by being supportive and resourceful, and by holding you accountable to progress.

A recent study from Ohio State University supports this idea, especially when it comes to articulating goals to supervisors and other influential people in your life.[45] Their research found that sharing your goals with someone whose opinion you value helps you achieve your goal more than keeping your goal to yourself.[46]

"Contrary to what you may have heard, in most cases you get more benefit from sharing your goal than if you don't— as long as you share it with someone whose opinion you value," said Howard Klein, the lead author of the study and a professor of management and human resources at The Ohio State University's Fisher College of Business.[47]

Other studies affirm the positive benefits of sharing goals, connecting that activity with higher motivation, self-confidence, and autonomy.[48] Formulating and writing down your goals is another step you can take to ensure fulfillment of those goals. Writing down your goals helps you clarify them, leaves no room for misinterpretation, and creates an ongoing self-reminder.[49]

However, a Harvard Business Review article recommends approaching goal setting carefully—especially goals that may seem unattainable:[50] "On the bright side, the persistent pursuit of unattainable goals can lead to higher achievements. People who suspected beforehand that a goal was unattainable may later think, 'If I didn't attempt that goal, I would have achieved a lot less than what I have now. So, I'm much better off for having tried.'"[51]

"Focusing on smaller accomplishments can bolster positive feelings, motivating us to take on more goals in the same category," the article continued. "As long as we know that unattainable goals are not really about the destination, but the journey, they can be quite healthy. On the dark side, unattainable goals often end in failures and how people react to failure varies greatly. For some, especially those who put a great deal of time and effort into a long-shot goal, failure can be a crushing blow. If not managed well, fixating on the fact that one failed may lead to negative self-fulfilling prophecies or self-critical thinking. Prolonged thoughts like these can lead to a psychological downward spiral."[52]

My Personal and Professional Goal-Setting Journey

I realized that throughout my life, I shared my goals, dreams, ambitions, and aspirations with my family, friends, and colleagues. Here are just a few examples that I had set in my professional life and shared with others:

- Earn a six-figure income by the time I am 25
- Achieve a VP role before age 30
- Achieve the number one office in the company
- Achieve the number one region in the company
- Become a president of business
- Become a millionaire
- Sit on an Advisory Board
- Write a book – *Finally!*

Over the years, I also shared many personal goals with others. These were more focused on fun, fitness, and livelihood. Sharing and vocalizing my goals helped me achieve many aspirations. It kept me on track and focused on what was important to me. Here are those goals:

- Buy my first house
- Buy a house on the water
- Own a vacation home on the water
- Run a marathon
- Complete a triathlon
- Take the kids to Disney World

- Travel to Europe
- Own a fancy convertible sports car (mid-life crisis)

Yes, some of these things are material items—but they were still goals I set for myself. I also had other meaningful goals like:

- Make contributions and donations to schools to increase safety and promote innovation and technology advancements
- Volunteer to teach religious education and strengthen my faith
- Mentor and coach other women to achieve their dreams
- Volunteer my time to talk with children/students about careers and careers of the future

I set my sights high for myself and for those around me. I always will. I like to create plans to achieve my goals and aspirations, but I also offer up positive energy and encouragement to all those around me. I discuss things with my family and friends, and I verbally commit to them. I speak up, and I encourage everyone to do the same. Let your intentions and desires be known to others. Most people are good-natured and want to see you achieve your desires. They want to pay good deeds forward and be supportive. Give people the benefit of the doubt. Let them help you.

Bottom line ... speak up! If you don't, you will limit your chances of achieving and getting what you want in life.

My American Staffing Association Journey

After a rewarding experience serving on the board of the American Staffing Association for a year, I got another call from Richard.

"Hello Joanie!" Richard said as I answered the phone.

"Richard, great to hear from you," I replied. "How can I help you?"

"You've done a great job during your first year on the board," he said. "We've just had an officer spot become available, and I think you'd be a great addition to our officers of the board. I'm calling to ask if you would consider a nomination for a term starting next year."

"That's amazing. I'm honored you would ask me after one year on the board." I replied.

"Let me tell you a bit more about what it involves," he said. "You'd serve on the finance committee, which requires more time than you've needed to devote so far. As a new officer, you'd make a five-year commitment that would eventually culminate in becoming the chairman of the organization."

"It does sound like a big commitment."

"Yes," he said. "I want to make sure you know what you're getting into. That said, I'm fully confident that you can handle it. You'd be a fantastic addition to serving as an officer. Why don't you give it some thought and get back to me in the next few days."

While I gave the matter serious consideration, I never thought about turning the offer down. I knew I had the bandwidth to stretch a bit more and the support of my employer. Of course, I eventually accepted, and I have loved the experience so far.

The American Staffing Association truly makes a difference in the staffing and recruiting industry. They protect and support the staffing industry with legal and legislative matters, provide thought leadership, and ultimately help more people get back to work. I look forward to serving as a chairperson of the American Staffing Association, and I will continue to contribute to such an incredibly rewarding industry that has provided me with such a wonderful career. The industry makes a difference in millions of lives, and it has afforded others and me a wonderful and rewarding career path. I am thankful I "dove" headfirst into this industry over 25 years ago.

I know in my heart that had I not spoken up and shared my intentions with others, I would not be where I am today. I can't stress enough the importance of speaking up to advance your career and reach new heights.

Reaching New Heights

This past year, I chose the word "reach" as my word of the year. "Reach" has multiple meanings for me on a professional and personal level. I am reaching to achieve new heights in growing my business, and my team even created a theme of "reach" initiatives to accomplish our goals and objectives. I am focused on increasing my reach in how I connect and communicate with others, including helping others achieve their goals, advance their careers, and live their best lives. I am also reaching to improve my own physical and emotional well-being.

My hope is that this book has made you think about reaching new heights in your career and in your life. I hope it helps you reach a new level of balance and harmony. I hope it helps you think about climbing to the higher diving platforms in your life and encourages you to dive in. To feel the fear and dive in anyway. You can achieve more than you can ever dream of if you are willing to put in the effort and work ethic. Stay true to yourself, and don't stop dreaming of what's next.

So, what's next for me? Though I am proud of my accomplishments, there is more I want to achieve. I want to continue to grow and expand my role and my business, but I have a few other things on my bucket list too. I am focused on supporting my kids to complete their college degrees and launch their careers. I'm looking forward to some amazing travel and trips over the next few years. I have created a long list of places I want to visit and see. I still have some big dreams, and I am not done climbing the diving platforms just yet.

We can design our careers and lives in a way that offers us higher satisfaction, fulfillment, balance, joy, and success. Dive into yourself and follow the D.E.E.P. process to reach your potential and aspirations: Design, Experience, Execute and Persevere.

Just as my dad encouraged me to dive into the deep end of the pool as a child, I encourage you to Dive in D.E.E.P. to yourself, your career, and all your ambitions. We only have one life to live, so why not make the most of it?

What are you waiting for? Take a D.E.E.P. Dive into you!

CHAPTER FIFTEEN REFLECTION

When you share your dreams and desires with others, you get one step closer to bringing them to fruition. There is something magical about verbalizing your goals and ambitions with others. When you share your ambitions with others, you are verbally committing to your goals. Tell others *what* you want to do and *how* you plan to get there. We can design our careers and lives in a way that offers us higher satisfaction, fulfillment, balance, joy, and success. Don't be afraid to speak up. Dive into yourself and follow the D.E.E.P. process to reach your potential and aspirations: Design, Experience, Execute and Persevere!

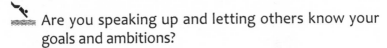 Are you speaking up and letting others know your goals and ambitions?

What areas in life do you want to reach higher and further?

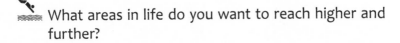 Are you taking calculated risks and learning from mistakes?

 How can you advocate for yourself and share your ambitions?

How can you leverage coaches and mentors to help refine your skills and learn new techniques?

FINAL REFLECTIONS

I began this book by sharing the significance of foundations and the importance of testing the waters and experiencing different industries and opportunities. I shared recommendations on how to leverage stretch assignments, mentors, internships, and early work experience. Experience is the key here. Think of experiences as tools that you continue to put in your toolbox. You will carry these tools throughout your career, and they will help you become an experienced craftsman in your field. You will gain knowledge and wisdom with each experience. And hopefully you will always be open to learning new things at each stage. These tools will give you the ability to execute on your plans and dreams.

The D.E.E.P. process is meant to be followed many times in life. This isn't something we go through one time and master. I have followed it numerous times as I have evaluated new goals or objectives for myself. Maybe you are beginning a new phase in life or want to learn a new skill or trade. It is never too early, and it is never too late to follow your dreams.

The process of goal setting can help you achieve your dreams and live the life you desire. I have faith you can achieve anything you set your mind to if you are willing to put in the D.E.E.P. work to make it happen. Remember to persevere through the belly flops, obstacles, and challenges. You can learn the most through these times and I believe everything happens for a reason. There are lessons and learnings in all the hardship.

In summary, I wanted to offer some final coaching tips for your career and life:

Tip 1 – Never stop learning. Knowledge and experiences will improve the way you think, act, and make decisions. You will refine your skills. Commit to becoming a lifelong learner and trying new things. Take online classes and read industry-related articles and publications.

Tip 2 – Find purpose and make a difference. Years ago, I worked with an executive recruiter who would always focus on what someone made, saved, or achieved for an organization. He would write M.S.A. on the top of a candidate's resume to illustrate this. What had this person made, saved, and achieved? So, what's your M.S.A.? What can you make, save, or achieve in life?

Tip 3 – Welcome and invite feedback. No one expects you to be an expert in the beginning of your career. It takes time, training, practice, learning, and experience to refine your expertise. One of the best pieces of advice I can give you is to welcome and invite feedback on how you are performing. Some people may be intimidated to ask for feedback, but I encourage you to seek it out. People will admire your open mind and ability to handle constructive criticism. You will refine your skills and increase your effectiveness.

Tip 4 – Be confidently humble. Be someone who contributes and works well alongside their peers. It is important to pull your weight and be a team player. Make sure you are contributing to the teams' goals and priorities. Be generous with your efforts, time, and with sharing your knowledge.

Tip 5 – Don't settle. Find better. You deserve the opportunity to achieve your dreams and live your best life. Don't accept mediocrity—you will regret it if you do. Make a bucket list and go for it! If you are in the wrong job or wrong relationship, then make a plan and put in the work required to make the change. You owe it to yourself.

Design the career and life you wish to achieve and which you deserve. Keep Dreaming BIG! Gain experiences to learn, grow, and develop your expertise. Practice and refine your skills. Don't be afraid to make mistakes or belly flop occasionally. We grow and learn the most from our failures, which serve as valuable lessons. Embrace and embody the value of a strong work ethic and accountability. Train, practice, and build a strong reputation in all you do. Stay true to your goals, yourself, and your desires. Persevere through trials and tribulations to achieve success. Don't let anyone tell you that you can't accomplish something. Go all-out and give your best efforts. You are worth it.

ENDNOTES

1. "Employees Seek Personal Value and Purpose At Work. Be Prepared to Deliver," Gartner, January 13, 2022, https://www.gartner.com/en/articles/employees-seek-personal-value-and-purpose-at-work-be-prepared-to-deliver

2. "Help Your Employees Find Purpose – Or Watch them Leave," McKinsey, April 5, 2021, https://www.mckinsey.com/business-functions/organization/our-insights/help-your-employees-find-purpose-or-watch-them-leave

3. "Elevating the Workforce Experience: The Work Relationship," Deloitte, March 21, 2021, https://www2.deloitte.com/us/en/blog/human-capital-blog/2021/the-value-of-meaningful-work-to-workers.html

4. "Why Your Values Belong at Work," Harvard Business Review, Jan. 21, 2021, https://hbr.org/2021/01/why-your-values-belong-at-work

5. "Why Your Values Belong at Work," Harvard Business Review, Jan. 21, 2021, https://hbr.org/2021/01/why-your-values-belong-at-work

6. "Purpose: A Practical Guide," LinkedIn, 2016, https://business.linkedin.com/content/dam/me/business/en-us/talent-solutions/resources/pdfs/Practical-Guide-to-Purpose-at-Work.pdf

7. "The Workplace: A Place of Purpose," Work Design Magazine, January 2021, https://www.workdesign.com/2021/01/the-workplace-a-place-of-purpose/

8. "Barrett Values Assessment," Barrett Values Centre, 2021, https://www.valuescentre.com

9. "How Often Do People Change Jobs During a Lifetime?" TheBalance.com, June 15, 2020, https://www.thebalancecareers.com/how-often-do-people-change-jobs-2060467

10. "About Us," Spanx.com, 2021, https://www.spanx.com/about-us

11 "About Us," Spanx.com, 2021, https://www.spanx.com/about-us

12 "The Limping Giant: The American Economy 1974-75, the Federal Reserve Bank of Minneapolis, Jan. 1, 1975, https://www.minneapolisfed.org/article/1975/the-limping-giant-the-american-economy-197475

13 "Unemployment Rate by Year Since 1929 Compared to Inflation and GDP," TheBalance.com, March 21, 2021, https://www.thebalance.com/unemployment-rate-by-year-3305506

14 "The future of work after COVID-19," McKinsey Global Institute, February 18, 2021, https://www.mckinsey.com/featured-insights/future-of-work/the-future-of-work-after-covid-19

15 "Fastest declining occupations," U.S. Bureau of Labor Statistics, 2019, https://www.bls.gov/emp/tables/fastest-declining-occupations.htm

16 "Blockbuster Could Have Bought Netflix for $50 Million, but the CEO Thought It was a Joke," Inc.com, Sept. 20, 2019, https://www.inc.com/minda-zetlin/netflix-blockbuster-meeting-marc-randolph-reed-hastings-john-antioco.html

17 "These are the top 10 job skills of tomorrow—and long it takes to learn them," The World Economic Forum, Oct. 21, 2020, https://www.weforum.org/agenda/2020/10/top-10-work-skills-of-tomorrow-how-long-it-takes-to-learn-them/

18 "Defining the skills citizens will need in the future world of work," McKinsey, June 25, 2021, https://www.mckinsey.com/industries/public-and-social-sector/our-insights/defining-the-skills-citizens-will-need-in-the-future-world-of-work

19 "These are the top 10 job skills of tomorrow—and long it takes to learn them," The World Economic Forum, Oct. 21, 2020, https://www.weforum.org/agenda/2020/10/top-10-work-skills-of-tomorrow-how-long-it-takes-to-learn-them/

20 "These are the top 10 job skills of tomorrow—and long it takes to learn them," The World Economic Forum, Oct. 21, 2020, https://www.weforum.org/agenda/2020/10/top-10-work-skills-of-tomorrow-how-long-it-takes-to-learn-them/

21 "Mentoring Statistics: The Research You Need to Know," Guider, Feb. 3, 2020, https://www.guider-ai.com/blog/mentoring-statistics-the-research-you-need-to-know

22 "Mentoring Statistics: The Research You Need to Know," Guider, Feb. 3, 2020, https://www.guider-ai.com/blog/mentoring-statistics-the-research-you-need-to-know

23 "Mentoring Statistics: The Research You Need to Know," Guider, Feb. 3, 2020, https://www.guider-ai.com/blog/mentoring-statistics-the-research-you-need-to-know

24 "Mentoring Statistics: The Research You Need to Know," Guider, Feb. 3, 2020, https://www.guider-ai.com/blog/mentoring-statistics-the-research-you-need-to-know

25 "2021 Future of Recruiting Study," Career Arc, 2021, https://explore.careerarc.com/future-of-recruiting?mkt_tok=MjYyLUlDTC04MjgAAAGB9NKNWeaoHM_HEAfnR7v0DQy_YsFuf5kK4ttfySJRdCN46IIvZCzLGdHHpHl3jv3cdi2PT75LXQR3FzPXqyHDdulGIORkW4T8o1sctz0Wf1AsKQ

26 "2021 Future of Recruiting Study," Career Arc, 2021, https://explore.careerarc.com/future-of-recruiting?mkt_tok=MjYyLUlDTC04MjgAAAGB9NKNWeaoHM_HEAfnR7v0DQy_YsFuf5kK4ttfySJRdCN46IIvZCzLGdHHpHl3jv3cdi2PT75LXQR3FzPXqyHDdulGIORkW4T8o1sctz0Wf1AsKQ

27 "Future of Work Report 2022," Monster.com, Jan. 26, 2021, https://www.prnewswire.com/news-releases/monster-announces-the-results-of-2021-future-of-work-survey-301215440.html

28 "2021 Recruiter National Report," Jobvite.com, September, 2021, https://www.jobvite.com/wp-content/uploads/2021/09/Jobvite-RecruiterNation-Report-WEB-2.pdf

29 "2021 Recruiter National Report," Jobvite.com, September, 2021, https://www.jobvite.com/wp-content/uploads/2021/09/Jobvite-RecruiterNation-Report-WEB-2.pdf

30 "Meet Amanda Gorman: The History-Making Poet the World is Still Talking About," Reader's Digest, April 27, 2021, https://www.rd.com/article/who-is-amanda-gorman/

31 "Amanda Gorman Tells Oprah Winfrey Why Her Speech Impediment is 'One of my Greatest Strengths,'" People Magazine, March 25, 2021, https://people.com/human-interest/amanda-gorman-opens-up-speech-impediment-oprah-winfrey-interview/

32 "Amanda Gorman Captures the Moment, in Verse," The New York Times, Jan. 19, 2021, https://www.nytimes.com/2021/01/19/books/amanda-gorman-inauguration-hill-we-climb.html

33 "Wordsmith. Change-maker," TheAmandaGorman.com, https://www.theamandagorman.com

34 "Amanda Gorman," Poets.org, https://poets.org/poet/amanda-gorman

35 "Hiya, Gorgeous," KrisCarr.com, https://kriscarr.com/meet-kris/

36 "16 Wildly Successful People Who Overcame Huge Obstacles To Get There, HuffPost, Sept. 25, 2013, https://www.huffpost.com/entry/successful-people-obstacles_n_3964459

37 "Meet Kris," KrisCarr.com, https://kriscarr.com/meet-kris/

38 "2022 Gender Diversity Index Report," 50/50 Women on Boards, September 2022, https://www.prnewswire.com/news-releases/5050-women-on-boards-annual-gender-diversity-index-study-reveals-the-pace-is-slowing-for-women-joining-boards-however-when-women-lead-boards-are-more-diverse-301636330.html

39 "2022 Gender Diversity Index Report," 50/50 Women on Boards, September 2022, https://www.prnewswire.com/news-releases/5050-women-on-boards-annual-gender-diversity-index-study-reveals-the-pace-is-slowing-for-women-joining-boards-however-when-women-lead-boards-are-more-diverse-301636330.html

40 "Board Diversity in 2021," Mogul, https://get.onmogul.com/boards/

41 "Critical Mass on Corporate Boards: Why Three or More Women Enhance Governance," Wellesley Centers for Women," 2006, https://www.wcwonline.org/vmfiles/CriticalMassExecSummary.pdf

42 "Women on Boards," Yale School of Management, 2022, https://som.yale.edu/executive-education/for-individuals/leadership/women-on-boards

43 "Gender Diversity at the Board Level Can Mean Innovation Success," MITSloan Management Review, Jan. 22, 2020, https://sloanreview.mit.edu/article/gender-diversity-at-the-board-level-can-mean-innovation-success/

44 "Lean In: Women, Work and the Will to Lead," LeanIn.org, https://leanin.org/book#!

45 "Share your goals – but be careful whom you tell," Ohio State University, Sept. 3, 2019, https://news.osu.edu/share-your-goals--but-be-careful-whom-you-tell/

46 "Share your goals – but be careful whom you tell," Ohio State University, Sept. 3, 2019, https://news.osu.edu/share-your-goals--but-be-careful-whom-you-tell/

47 "Share your goals – but be careful whom you tell," Ohio State University, Sept. 3, 2019, https://news.osu.edu/share-your-goals--but-be-careful-whom-you-tell/

48 "The Science & Psychology of Goal Setting 101," Positive Psychology.com, Aug. 12, 2021, https://positivepsychology.com/goal-setting-psychology/

49 "Why Writing Down Your Goals Can Help You Achieve Them," SelfDevelopmentSecrets.com, https://www.selfdevelopmentsecrets.com/writing-down-your-goals/

50 "Why We Set Unattainable Goals," Harvard Business Review, Jan. 4, 2021. https://hbr.org/2021/01/why-we-set-unattainable-goals

51 "Why We Set Unattainable Goals," Harvard Business Review, Jan. 4, 2021. https://hbr.org/2021/01/why-we-set-unattainable-goals

52 "Why We Set Unattainable Goals," Harvard Business Review, Jan. 4, 2021. https://hbr.org/2021/01/why-we-set-unattainable-goals

CPSIA information can be obtained
at www.ICGtesting.com
Printed in the USA
LVHW051229120523
746812LV00004B/610